MOTHER ANGELICA'S LITTLE BOOK OF LIFE LESSONS AND EVERYDAY SPIRITUALITY

MOTHER ANGELICA'S LITTLE BOOK OF LIFE LESSONS AND EVERYDAY SPIRITUALITY

EDITED AND WITH ADDITIONAL
MATERIAL BY

RAYMOND ARROYO

WALKER LARGE PRINT
A part of Gale, Cengage Learning

GALE
CENGAGE Learning

Detroit • New York • San Francisco • New Haven, Conn • Waterville, Maine • London

GALE
CENGAGE Learning

LIBRARY OF CONGRESS CATALOGING-IN-PUBLICATION DATA

M. Angelica (Mary Angelica), Mother, 1923–
   Mother Angelica's little book of life lessons and everyday
spirituality / edited and with additional material by Raymond
Arroyo. — Large print ed.
    p. cm.
   ISBN-13: 978-0-7862-9916-4 (hardcover : alk. paper)
   ISBN-10: 0-7862-9916-9 (hardcover : alk. paper)
   ISBN-13: 978-1-59415-220-7 (softcover : alk. paper)
   ISBN-10: 1-59415-220-9 (softcover : alk. paper)
   1. Spirituality. 2. Spiritual life — Christianity. 3. Christian life.
4. Large type books. I. Arroyo, Raymond. II. Title. III. Title:
Little book of life lessons and everyday spirituality.
BV4501.3.M192 2008
248.4'82—dc22   2007036544

Published in 2008 by arrangement with Doubleday,
a division of Random House, Inc.

Printed in the United States of America
1 2 3 4 5 6 7 12 11 10 09 08

FOR MY LITTLE ONES:
Mariella, Lorenzo, and Alexander

AND FOR MOTHER'S:
The Poor Clares of Perpetual Adoration
at
Our Lady of the Angels Monastery,
The Franciscan Missionaries of the
Eternal Word,
and
Her spiritual children, the world over

Thou hast hidden these things from the wise and prudent, and hast revealed them to little ones. Yea, Father, for so it hath seemed good in Thy sight.

— Luke 10:21

CONTENTS

INTRODUCTION

When she first saw the plump Franciscan nun on TV, Markie Works wanted to flip the channel. "Oh forget this," she told herself on a Chicago night in April of 2001. But as she reached past the empty beer bottles for the remote, something about the nun held her attention.

Markie was routinely using drugs at the time and ending her evenings with a succession of nightcaps. Considering all the woman had lived through, one could hardly blame her. Markie was eighteen months old when her mother was fatally shot in the head by an uncle. Abuse and a series of bad choices had led her to the fleeting comforts found in thin white lines of powder and at the bottom of a shot glass.

Earlier that week, her physical and emotional condition had so deteriorated that Markie had begged God to take her life, or rescue her from the life she had been living.

Then she happened across this nun.

Mother Angelica was responding to a viewer, near the end of her live call-in show. The despondent caller had been mistreated and rejected by her mother all her life. After sympathetically listening, the straight-talking nun in her espresso-tinted habit leaned forward, looked with genuine concern into the camera lens, and said: "It's all right honey. I'll be your mother now."

Markie began bawling. Something in the nun's demeanor, something so honest, so real, touched her wounded heart. It was as if Mother Angelica was speaking directly to her. The bottled-up pain she carried over the loss of her mother, the wretched choices, the misery of her present condition spilled out in a cleansing torrent of tears. In that moment, Angelica became Markie's spiritual mother. Her problems didn't vanish, but she immediately realized that she "no longer had to carry the cross alone."

She began tuning in to *Mother Angelica Live* each week, and slowly found her way out of the despair that had consumed her life. Today Markie is free of drugs and alcohol, has a family, and is deeply grateful to Mother Angelica for the spiritual guidance, and the teachings that got her through the dark times. She is not alone.

One could say that Angelica, or Rita Rizzo, as she was known before religious life, was a mother from early childhood. By the age of seven she was already providing emotional support and protection to her birth mother, Mae Rizzo. Her father, John, had walked out on the family when Rita was only five.

Singed by the fires of abandonment and disability, she learned at a tender age to rely on God alone. This difficult background and the time spent in prayer as a contemplative nun would acutely shape the later teachings of Mother Angelica. In her lessons, she sought to apply traditional Christian spirituality to the confused, complex world she knew all too well. Her teachings pulsed with a practical simplicity, an earthy humor, and a beguiling wisdom that would draw many eyes and hearts.

For nearly three decades, Mother Angelica, speaking the language of the common man, used every form of the media to spread her message of hope to the masses. In 1972, she founded a print shop, where her nuns published millions of her spiritual "mini books." Following the example of her Divine Spouse, she traversed the countryside delivering inspiring, often uproarious, talks on the spiritual life. And in 1981, at fifty-eight years of age, against all odds, she built the largest religious media empire on the planet, The Eternal Word Television Network (EWTN) — which would make hers a household name.

Mother would continue teaching millions until a massive stroke hit her on Christmas Eve, 2001, limiting her speech and effectively ending her public career. Still, she remains a cultural force.

Today she can be seen and heard in reruns on cable television, AM/FM, satellite and shortwave radio, the Internet, and even on your iPod. Yet for all her renown, there existed no single volume which preserved her remarkable spirit and provided a full sampling of her major teachings. Mother Angelica, her nuns, and I believed this omission should be corrected.

Throughout the book tour for my biography, *Mother Angelica, the Remarkable Story of a Nun, Her Nerve, and a Network of Miracles,* I can't tell you how often people waited on line to share how Mother's story or words had transformed their lives. Misty-eyed CEOs, lawyers, maids, truck drivers, and home-schooling moms stood in queues to pay tribute to her, and to ask questions, sometimes very pointed questions: How can I find God's will in my life as Mother did?

How can I pray more deeply? How can I overcome the faults that seem to be holding my life hostage? How did Mother find the strength to cope with all the suffering she experienced?

You hold in your hands the answers to these universal questions, and many more.

If my biography was the body of Mother's life, this is its lifeblood. Herein are the beliefs, teachings, life lessons, wit, and prayers that sustained Angelica's incredible journey.

Many of the quotes that follow have not been heard since Mother first uttered them. They are drawn primarily from her live appearances before secular and church groups, a Bible study conducted in her monastery parlor for an ecumenical guild of women in the early 1970s, private lessons given to her nuns over a thirty-year period, and interviews with me from 1999–2001. Through a special collaborative agreement, Mother Angelica and her monastery gave me unprecedented access to materials thought lost, and many transcriptions and recordings never seen or heard by the public.

Believing that there is power in things done or said the first time, I opted to go back to the earliest teachings of Mother Angelica and to trace their evolution. Hers was a lively art. As she turned to inspiration for the bold strokes that would define her life, so she would rely upon it to lend expression and cogency to her teachings. While confronting real-world concerns and questions before live audiences, whether her nuns or the public, Mother Angelica would coin new phrases and give shape to the original yet timeless philosophy she would call on again and again. The distillation of her initial creativity would appear decades later on her television programs. But those early efforts, when she was still refining her message, contain an improvisatory crackle, a vibrancy and passion that rival even her best television work. The final selections here capture her ideas and advice at both the moment of their inception and, in some cases, after years of fermentation. All are pithy, insightful, and so relevant.

Rather than getting lost in the speculative concepts and theological hairsplitting that is the business of others, Angelica offers practical, everyday spiritual answers to lay-people in distress. The solutions are not always easy, but they are doable.

In some ways this work is like a sit-down with Mother Angelica; a chance to soak up the wisdom and joy of a woman who has lived a life of indomitable faith. This little book is broken into digestible chapters that the reader may dip into for a quick infusion of inspiration, or can be used as a continual devotional for daily spiritual reflection. But be forewarned, this is a devotional like none other. Once you plunge in, your spirit may be as agitated as your funny bone. Don't say you weren't warned.

During her public life, Mother Angelica taught that holiness did not require perfection (welcome news for many of us), that all are eligible, and that we need not check our temperaments or personalities at the door of sanctity. She burned with an intense love for the person and message of Jesus Christ, and attempted to impart that passion to others. She showed normal folks how to tap into God's power each day, and how to humbly accept His will in the Present Moment. Her simple, no-nonsense approach to spirituality and daily living is so needed today. So here it is, unvarnished and accessible.

In this world of bloated egos and overinflated hype, Mother Angelica once told me she considered herself "a porcupine at a balloon party." May you find strength and refreshment in her quills. And here's hoping you get skewered once or twice along the way.

Raymond Arroyo
Loudon County, Virginia
Feast of the Assumption, 2006

OPENING PRAYER

Lord God, we bless Your Holy Name.

We ask You, Omnipotent Lord, to guide us,

and grant those who read this book many, many graces.

Most of all, let us reveal Your infinite wisdom,

Your knowledge, Your understanding, Your Providence,

Your goodness, Your mercy, and how much You

plan our lives, or wish to plan them.

Grant that this work may manifest to Thy people Your

constant care for them, and show how You have arranged

every moment for them, every instant of their lives.

Teach them to be docile to Your Will; for behind that

Will are great things in this life and in the next.

For this we ask Thy blessing and aid. Amen.

COMPOSED BY MOTHER ANGELICA

1
Eternal
Perspectives

The Beginning of the End

Mother Angelica fervently believed in maintaining an eternal perspective for everyday living; a constant awareness that we must account for our actions in this life, and that a final judgment awaits each of us. Of course she put it more succinctly:

Everyone drags his own carcass to market. So be careful.

God Loves You

I didn't know God loved me for a long time. Many feel that way. Because we are so aware of our faults, our weaknesses, our sins, we have an impression that God couldn't love us. Well that's not true. God is infinite. There is no end to His love. He doesn't love you for anything you possess. He loves you because He is love. We're all imperfect.

We're all sinners, and many of us would be much worse than we are given the opportunity.

Seeing God

It is easier to see God in the sinner because I must make an effort to do so. It is one of the paradoxes of life that I run the risk of losing sight of God in those who are easy to love, because I begin to seek my own good in them.

Little Things

God chooses little things to do big things.

God Chose You

God knew you, loved you, and chose you before there was an angel, before there was a world, a universe or a star.

This Life

You have to enjoy life without resting in it. You have to have zest for life but a desire for heaven. And you must see God in all things, realizing that He transcends them all.

HUMILITY

Ask yourselves: How little am I before God? Am I poor in spirit? Do I accept my weaknesses, my past, my sins, my idiosyncrasies, my eccentricities, and my failures? Do I accept them cheerfully? To accept one's miserable self, cheerfully, is humility.

THE WAY TO HEAVEN

You must laugh your way to heaven, because tears won't get you there.

CRACKED POTS

The Scripture says, "We are only earthenware jars" (2 Cor. 4:7). Cracked pots! That's what you are, a cracked pot that holds this great treasure. We are, all of us, imperfect, but we must remember that the Spirit of God is inside each of us.

MYSTERY AND FAITH

St. Augustine, one of our greatest minds in the Church, was walking on the seashore and he saw a little child. While he was walking, he tried to comprehend the Trinity: how there could possibly be three persons in one God. Further down the shore, this little child kept scooping a bucket of water and pouring it into a little hole on the beach. St.

Augustine watched the child run back and forth, trying to fill the hole with water. Finally he said, "Son, what are you doing?"

The boy just looked at Augustine and said, "I'm trying to put the ocean in this hole."

"You can't. That's impossible," Augustine said.

"Neither can you understand the Trinity," the child responded. Then he disappeared.

So remember when you come upon a mystery — either in your life, or in Scripture, or in the life of Jesus — your mind can't accommodate all that is contained in the infinite, Holy God. Kinda like trying to put the entire ocean in a small hole, isn't it?

SUNKEN TREASURE

The riches of heaven are the things we should be desirous of — not the things of the world. The only treasures we know are the sunken variety. We've all seen those movies where the pirates open the trunks filled with diamonds and rubies, and we know there is tons of stuff buried at sea. It shows you what God thinks of them — they're down at the bottom! God's concept of treasure is a soul that deeply loves Him and deeply loves its neighbor. That invisible reality is far more valuable than the passing trinkets of this world.

GOD'S CHOICE

God is not hindered if He wants to use you, whether you are holy, perfect, imperfect, good or bad. He can speak through an ass if He wants to. And He did. Remember, that's how He spoke to Balaam the prophet (Num. 22:28–30). So there is hope for all of us.

SPEAKING THE TRUTH

We don't like to speak the truth about evil because we're going to hurt somebody. Let me tell you, you are going to hurt somebody, but that Somebody is God. If you would rather hurt God than your neighbor, there is something wrong with your spirituality. It's your obligation to speak the truth and everyone can either take it or leave it. But truth must be in us. We live in such poverty of the truth today.

THAT OTHER COMMANDMENT

Boldness should be the eleventh commandment!

MAKING DEALS WITH GOD

In 1957 Mother Angelica faced a hazardous spinal operation. The night before the procedure, the surgeon informed Angelica that she had only a fifty-fifty chance of ever walking again. She prayed zealously that night and made a pact with God. She told Him, "If You allow me to walk again I will build a monastery to Your glory in the South." With the aid of crutches and several braces, she did walk again. From then on she would advise:

"When you make a deal with God be *very* specific."

FEAR NOTHING

When you have Jesus, what is there to fear?

LOOKING FOR DUMMIES

The apostles were dodos, dummies. But all the smart people in the world at the time wouldn't take chances. That is the same problem we have today. The world is looking for intellectuals and the Lord is looking for dummies. That's why I'm here.

A MASTER'S DEGREE

We're all trying to get master's degrees, and so often we forget the Master.

THE DEGREE THAT MATTERS

Where most men work for degrees after their names, we work for one before our names: "St." It's a much more difficult degree to attain. It takes a lifetime, and you don't get your diploma until you're dead.

LEADERS LIKE YOU

Who was Jesus looking for in His apostles — to be the leader of the leaders? Simple sinners, just like us. He looked for men who loved much, whose love made them un-afraid, and whose love never put a stop to God's grace. When Jesus said, "Go out without scrip or shoes" (Luke 10:4), they were dumb enough to go — they were loving enough to go.

ONE PERSON

Everything starts with one person. God loves to work with weak people — like David, a little teenager with a slingshot defeated the fearsome Goliath. Gideon with only three hundred men saved the Jewish people from slaughter and slavery. I don't care if you're five or one hundred and five, God from all eternity chose you to be where you are, at this time in history to change the world.

STEPPING OUT IN MYSTERY

We don't want to step out in faith and say, "God, the only hand I have is Yours, even though I don't know where You're going." I think that's the most thrilling experience: not to know what God is doing — but going out and doing it anyway.

It's very difficult for a real Christian to mess this up. If you try something and you fail, you've been humbled. You're a little smarter the next time; you learn to depend upon God and not yourself. You can learn much in failure. If you succeed: you are aware of God's spirit, aware of His using you in extraordinary ways. So from a spiritual perspective, you can't fail no matter what happens.

THE GREATEST POWER IN THE WORLD

The greatest power for good in this world is retarded children, the deaf, the dumb, and the blind — those who suffer loneliness. They have time to live with God, to experience the joy of God, to experience the presence of God, and their prayer is powerful before the Lord.

LIFE IS PASSING

No matter how successful one is, or how famous, there comes a time when he passes on. He's like a ship going through the ocean. The ship makes a little ripple, and

28

when it has passed through, the ocean closes in.

Isn't that what life is all about, each of us passing through? Why lament over the things you wanted and never got? Why lament over what could have been when it is all passing? Right now, you are not the person you were a half hour ago. We are one half hour closer to the journey's end. For some this is a distressing thought. Why is it that we find death so depressing? We can imagine everyone dying except ourselves. Have we lost sight of this world being a pilgrimage? It's a journey. You're not home yet. A Christian must never lose sight of this passing reality of life; and it should be faced with peace, not constant surprise.

GRUDGES

Don't waste your time in life trying to get even with your enemies. The grave is a tremendous equalizer. Six weeks after you all are dead, you'll look pretty much the same. Let the Lord take care of those whom you think have harmed you. All you have to do is love and forgive. Try to forget and leave all else to the Master.

FORGIVENESS

Forgiveness means "to give." It means to give before your neighbor does.

LIGHT AND FAITH

I believe if we want this world to stop going to hell, if we really want to do something about the darkness — then you have to light the light. There is no other way to banish darkness. You can sit in a dark room and fuss and complain about it, but all you have to do is turn on a light. God has placed us all in a dark room, hoping that we will have sense enough to turn the light on and not yell and scream and panic over the darkness, because we know where the light is — we know *who* the light is! And we have Him. The tragedy of this age will be if those who have the light do not let it shine. Christians of all denominations have literally put the light under a bushel.

HALF FED

Can you imagine our Lord today, in present-day Jerusalem, under such stressful conditions? Can you imagine Him getting up and saying: Blessed are the peacemakers? They would laugh Him to scorn. Because today, my friends, we only want to eat, drink, be merry, and grab all we can. "Don't talk to me about eternity, or love, or Jesus, or the Church. I want what I want — now! Give me bread now!" So we feed half the man, and then we wonder why he is empty.

GOOD ACTS

Don't kid yourself. The Lord sees every good act, every attempt you make to be holy. Many times, though we experience failure, He blesses our efforts. He sees it all: the kind words, the times you've held your tongue, or contained your anger. He keeps an eye on your heart, endlessly.

LOVING GOD

Since a stroke in 2001, Mother has been fairly quiet, speaking only when she has to. On March 22, 2006, one of the sisters asked Mother for a bit of wisdom. Without hesitating she said:

He who loves God loves everybody. He who hates God hates everybody.

2
YOUR MISSION, YOUR PURPOSE

"Who am I?" "Why am I here?" These fundamental questions, depending on the person, can take a lifetime to answer. As you might expect, Mother Angelica could answer them a lot quicker. Mission, purpose, and identity were bound together in Mother's thinking. She taught that it was far better to "find oneself" in proximity to God, than to attempt to do so separated from Him. After all, who knows the purpose of the creation better than the Creator?

Whether you are still finding your way in life or embarking on a new vocation, Mother has some guidance that will prove helpful now, and throughout the rest of your life.

THE CHRISTIAN VOCATION

The Christian vocation is simple: you are first a child of God, and the state of life where God has placed you is the source of your holiness.

Your True Identity

Everybody is searching for their identity. But the real you only emerges when you are united to God. You need His grace, and without it you are stumbling in darkness. Everybody wants to know who they are, where they're going, and what they're doing. Yet the realism of Heaven and God, that invisible reality, never enters the equation. Identity is *becoming*. It's an understanding of who you are, and why you were created by God. You can only understand it by knowing Him, because He has a very special plan for you. And that special plan makes its own demand: that you be faithful — faithful to the duties of your state of life.

Finding Yourself

You can't isolate yourself and say you want to "find yourself no matter what anyone else says or does." You'll never find yourself that way. You'll find a grotesque creature that you are creating as you go along. God made you in His image. He redeemed you so that you could reflect that image to your neighbor.

The thing that confuses us so much is that we are constantly thinking about ourselves: What am I going to do for the world? What am I going to do for my neighbor? You've got the wrong question.

The question is: What is God going to do through you? That's the question. How much are you going to let Him do? When you begin to ask the right questions you will get the right answers. You are nothing; and until you come to that realization, you will stumble and crawl through all of life. There is absolute freedom in the thought that you are nothing. Only then are you free to be used by God for His ends, the ends for which you have been created.

A MEDITATION ON YOUR CREATION

When I get a little discouraged in my own life, I like to make this meditation. I like to go back and visualize the Trinity before He created anything or anyone. Just God alone. In His mind, He knew everyone that He would create. And can you imagine God's eyes roaming over a possible 80 or 100 billion people who might have been. But they will never be. He passes them by, and suddenly His eyes rest on you. He says, "You shall be." Why you? Why me? If that were not enough, He placed you in a specific time, and of the billions of people on the planet only 1 billion would know His Son. And you were among that number. You must ask, "Why did You choose me, dear Lord, to know You and love You?" Because He loves you, and you can love Him in a way that no other creature in this whole wide world can love Him. You are that unique and special. Unless you understand this simple truth you will never love yourself or your neighbor.

THE BIG MISSION

You have been chosen twice: first to *be,* then to know Jesus. What are you doing with that fantastic mission? You have been created by God and know Jesus for one reason: to witness to faith, and hope, and love before an unbelieving world. I don't care if the world knows you, or no one knows you. Even if you influence only one person in your whole life, God does not look at numbers or quantities. He looks at souls and individuals. If you were able, by your example or by one of your acts, to bring one person to heaven, it would mean more to Him than all the accomplishments on earth.

THE PURPOSE OF CHRISTIANITY

The Father wants to look down and see His image on your soul. This is the purpose of Christianity.

MORE THAN A RELIGION

Christianity is much more than a religion. Religion is a pacifier. But Christianity is a way of life.

Christianity has become insipid, because we have become insipid. And this is why the world is the way it is.

CHANGE THE WORLD

Like the apostles, we Christians are arguing among ourselves when we should be out changing the world. We let filth proliferate and the darkness move in. Who do you think is going to change it? What are you waiting for? You are that somebody! The Lord God has no one else but you. You'd better get off your lead bottoms and go out there and change this pagan world.

THE DECISION

"This is a wicked age," the Scripture says, "your lives should redeem it" (Eph. 5:16). Well, you're not redeeming anything if you're lying and cheating and stealing and gossiping and committing adultery and getting drunk every Friday night. The reason we're not really Christian is we don't have the guts. We don't want to make a decision. Imagine the joy when you make a decision for Jesus, when you stand up for the Lord. Can you imagine the exaltation in the kingdom and the humiliation in the depths of hell when you, a puny, insignificant sinner, say no to the enemy and yes to God?

CHOICES FOR TRANSFORMATION

It's so important that you make the right choices now. Don't listen to the world, listen to the Eternal Word. Listen to the Church. Listen to your conscience. And make choices in favor of the Lord. Let us truly look at ourselves without fear. God knows us and He loves us as we are. But He also gives you the grace to be transformed — and that's the important thing in life.

FAITH

Faith is more than an intellectual assent to truth. It's something alive. Today we don't have a goal or a vision. And Jesus is asking you to have a vision. I don't mean you're going to see some saint or something. I mean a vision of what the whole world should be, what your family should be, your soul, and the whole Church.

THE PLAN OF LIFE

I want to live with God forever. That's my plan, and I hope it's yours too. How are you going to go to a God who is all-holiness, all-light, all-compassion, and all-mercy if you never tried to be any of those things? Is it hard? It sure is.

THE BEATITUDES: A BLUEPRINT FOR LIVING

If you build a house you have to have a blueprint. Everybody understands that. But in the spiritual life they forget it. And if you don't know the Beatitudes (Matt. 5:1–12), you don't know God's blueprint for your life.

The Lord said, *"Blessed are the poor in spirit: for theirs is the kingdom of Heaven."* Poverty of spirit is to be detached from the things of the world. You can have things or not have them. Some are so fastidious about the things they have that they refuse to let anyone use them; like a person who wraps their sofa in plastic, or when they get new carpet you have to enter through the back door.

You know, life is full of lemons. I learned

that when I bought a car. The poor in spirit don't mind the lemons in their lives. They recognize that nothing here is truly lasting. Even when a person who is poor in spirit desires something and doesn't get it, they are at peace because they know that things do not bring happiness. The depth of their spirit is with God and they possess a sense of serenity.

Next the Lord says, *"Blessed are the gentle: for they shall inherit the earth."* Our Lord was very gentle. The gentle think before they act. (I have to work on it and work hard. My Italian temperament was not meant to be gentle.) There is a peacefulness in a gentle person, a depth of compassion. They think of others first. Everyone loves a gentle person. It's hard to love a hothead.

Then the Lord adds: *"Blessed are those who mourn: for they shall be comforted."* Does that mean that everyone who goes to a funeral will be blessed? It has nothing to do with funerals. It means blessed are those who mourn over their sins. A lot of people don't mourn over their sins — heck, some people don't even know they have them. What our Dear Lord is saying is that when I mourn over my sins, He will comfort me. I am comforted when I go to confession. You see, the Beatitudes are multifaceted.

They are things of action, and things to be accomplished.

The Lord next says, *"Blessed are those who hunger and thirst for justice: for they shall be satisfied."* Do you hunger and thirst for goodness? Holiness? Do you hunger and thirst to see God? Have you ever longed in your heart to be rid of your sins and the inclinations toward sin? Have you ever thirsted for that freedom of a child of God? Our Lord promises you will be satisfied.

"Blessed are the merciful: for they shall have mercy shown them," Jesus says. We want mercy, but we don't want to give mercy. Why? I don't know. We just want those who hurt us to suffer a little bit. You ask the Father in heaven to forgive *you.* Now you must be willing to forgive others.

He adds, *"Blessed are the pure in heart: for they shall see God."* If you are not pure, your heart lusts after everything. Selfishness keeps you from being pure of heart. Most are so selfish; they don't care for anything except what is in it for them. You must love your neighbor for more than what he's going to do for you — and that, incidentally, is not love.

The Lord also tells us, *"Blessed are the peacemakers: for they shall be called sons of God."* He didn't say, "Blessed are the peace-

40

ful," He said, "Blessed are the peace-makers." You have to *make* peace. We should settle problems as soon as they start, keep our mouths shut, and pray for our enemies instead of gossiping about them. You have to work for the kingdom. It won't be easy, but do you want heaven or not?

Jesus then says, *"Blessed are those who are persecuted for a just cause: for theirs is the kingdom of heaven."* Wow, you are promised a lot. I like this next part, *"Blessed are you when people abuse you and persecute you and speak all kinds of calumny against you on my account. Rejoice and be glad, for your reward will be great in heaven; this is how they persecuted the prophets before you."* St. Luke's beatitude adds a little thing that I like, it reads: *"Rejoice when that day comes and dance for joy"* (Luke 6:23). I ought to be dancing all the time. Most people just want to drift placidly along, taking no stands, ruffling no feathers. Well this last beatitude tells us we have to rock the boat a bit. And remember, if you don't rock the boat no one will know how many holes it has in it.

You Are the Good News

This world is never going to see the Good News by reading the Good Book. Because they won't read it. They are only going to see it when you *live* it.

The Only Jesus

You may be the only Jesus your neighbor will ever see.

A Thorn

If you're not a thorn in somebody's side, you're not doing Christianity right.

Called by God

You are called by God at this time in history to be so holy that this whole world will be sanctified. And you're going to do that only by being yourself and changing that self into Jesus — cooperating with the Spirit to be transformed into the object of your love.

The One Goal Necessary

A Christian has one goal in mind: What does God want me to do? And he doesn't care what it costs, because he was not created for this life, but for the next.

WHAT GOD WANTS

There are only two things you have that God really wants: your will and your sins. Give your sins and imperfections to Him. He has come to call sinners, and once you respond, He will work with you.

THE BEST-LAID PLANS

I thought I'd live and die a little cloistered nun in a hidden monastery in Cleveland, Ohio — and that would be it. God had other plans. A little at a time, the Gentle Jesus unfolded His plans in my life as He unfolds them in yours. You're never alone. You must feel safe, always safe, and sure that whatever He does with you or for you, He can be trusted.

WHERE YOU ARE

We are all called to the place where God can use us the most. In my case, Our Dear Lord looked at me and said, "Kiddo, I've got to lock you up because that's the only place you can make it." I always say, the Lord spared some man a lifetime of trouble when He sent me to the cloister. I would have had him hopping, I can tell you . . .

A Quickie Prayer for the World

There's a beautiful ejaculation, a quickie prayer that Our Lord gave to Sister Maria Consolata Betrone. It says, "Jesus and Mary, I love you. Save souls." It's very simple but, oh, it carries a lot of weight. So intercede for the whole world.

A Want of Love

The whole world needs to hear two things with strength and power: "God loves you" and "I love you." You must say it often to your friends. This world is not starving from a lack of money. It's starving from a want of love.

It All Depends on You

God has willed that each of us give until there is nothing else to give. You see, all of creation, all the world, all mankind benefits or loses out because of you. You've got to understand what it means to love as Jesus loved.

The Power of Age

As we get older I sometimes wonder if we understand the power of the aged. We're not tapping that power. We're not tapping their experience or their wisdom. I wonder if we understand what God expects from us. It reminds me of the marriage at Cana where Jesus changed the water to wine. The steward said to Him, "You have kept the best wine until now." That's what age is. You know why? Because we have more time to say, "Jesus, I love you." At every moment of life I can love my neighbor, I can make a choice and choose God over the enemy. It gives you the opportunity to love and know God in a new way. Besides that, the holiness and the grace you are able to possess as you go from chains to transformation make you a witness to youth. Do not succumb to the concepts the world has of age. There is a dichotomy in our lives: I get older, but my soul is young — forever young. That's why it is so difficult to accept age: because my body is unable to do things as it used to, but my soul is so very young. On that beautiful day when I see Him face to face, I will have that same soul that I had when I was twenty or thirty, hopefully brighter and more like Him. The youth today need to look at you in your seventies and eighties and think, "The best wine is to come." But if you despair and are discouraged, what do they have to look forward to? See, our mission gets greater as we get older.

In the World, but Not of It

God wants you to be in the world, but so different from the world that you will change it. Get cracking.

Pressing Forward

Don't look back. St. Paul said, "I press forward." You and I have work to do, and we must do it together. Every man, woman, and child must know Jesus. God has created you with a fire, a spirit, to inflame others. You can no longer sit waiting for something to happen. You make it happen! You're the only one God has.

3
Living in the Present Moment

Among the most important themes in Mother Angelica's teaching was her constant plea to "live in the Present Moment." It dominated her approach to spirituality and was the overarching reason why she was so fearless in her pursuit of the mission given her by God. In these harried days, when we are so often stuck in the past or preoccupied with the future, Mother Angelica presents a different way, a superior way, to live and love.

Memory, Intellect, the Will, and the Past

I have within my soul faculties. My memory tells me who I am. My intellect tells me what I am. And my will tells me what I shall be. You must watch your memory and control it because it feeds your intellect, which in turn influences your will.

You see people today doing unreasonable things, and they do them because they are

living in their memories and imaginations
— they exist on an animal level. The intellect never comes into play. Self-control is one of the fruits of the Holy Spirit, which requires us to decide what enters our memory and what remains there. I must look upon every resentment, every bitterness, every hurt and conquer it, or it will conquer me.

We cannot permit the past to rule us. If you look at Jesus you will find that He never lived even for a moment on that base level. He expected his disciples to live on the faith level, in the Present Moment, at all times.

Remember when the apostles were terrified on the boat, the waves were breaking in and they were sinking. The Lord said, "Why are you so frightened, you men of little faith?" (Matt. 8:26). They were so afraid because they began to live on a memory level. Their previous experience told them that this type of storm would sink the ship. But what about God who is there in the Present Moment? Peter comes over and says, "Master, do you not care? We are going down!" (Mark 4:38). That's where he lost out.

Faith tells us the Lord is concerned with our welfare, always. The problem today is we play God in every aspect of our lives. We decide what He should do at every moment, and if He doesn't meet those expectations, then there is no God.

DANGEROUS LIVING IN THE PAST

Most people live in the past. When you find yourself alone you inevitably revisit the past. Recalling things that will help us in the Present Moment is fine. For instance, the alcoholic who recalls the fact that he can't have even one drink is necessary and helpful. It is the reliving of the past, the endless rehashing to the point where it affects your soul, that is dangerous.

Part of repentance is to remember your past sins and give your love to Jesus. But most people live in their past, in sin, guilt, remorse, resentment. They see every tiny detail related to those past events. They are actually living in that moment, and it's wrong. Because the moment you have now, this Present Moment, is all you have. You don't have the next moment, and the past is gone forever. But we keep bringing it back — "someone offended me," "someone said something" — and we keep reliving it in our minds over and over and over. You are then living in a moment that is gone, a fantasy.

This happens with glory too. You re-envision past successes in your life, past beauty. And you live in it so frequently that it becomes a reality for you — all the compliments, all the adulation. You are misusing a beautiful faculty, and it will warp your whole personality.

On the other hand, if you are living in a distasteful situation that happened last week or last month and someone comes to you needing your patience or charity, you're going to strike out at them with impatience and anger, even though they did nothing. You're not at home in the Present Moment. It paralyzes you, because you are not attuned to God and His love in this Present Moment.

LIVING IN THE FUTURE

We look into the future all the time, don't we? We imagine ourselves getting older, and we imagine we're going to have cancer, Alzheimer's, some terrible agony. We can feel the death rattle in our throats. We're going to get older and grayer and more wrinkled. Or you are experiencing a painful situation, and you envision it going on for another five or ten years. Soon you begin to live in that projected delusion. So instead of suffering one moment at a time, you have suffered ten years in a capsule. It's like a drama, it's like a soap opera on TV, and your mind keeps embellishing the pain. Some people say, "You've got to face reality." But that is not reality. That is a fantastic bubble of your own creation.

Our Lord says in the Gospel of St. Matthew: "I am telling you not to worry about your life and what you are to eat, nor about your body and how you are to clothe it" (Matt. 6:25). Now, is He saying don't eat and run around naked? The word *worry* means "to live in." He doesn't want you to live in the future.

Only God knows what your future will be — or even if you will have a future. Jesus has pleaded with us and shown us His example. He wants us to live just in this Present Moment. Do it. Now.

YOUR WHOLE LIFE IS NOW

In the Gospel of Matthew, the Lord tells us, "Set your hearts on His kingdom *first* and His righteousness, and all these other things will be given you as well. So do not worry about tomorrow" (Matt. 6:33–34). Now here is a sentence we forget entirely: "Tomorrow will take care of itself." Why? Because tomorrow will soon be *now!* Have you ever noticed that there really is never a

51

tomorrow? It's always *now. Your whole life is now.*

You know, people come to me and they consider their past life, and they say, "Oh, if I could just do the whole thing over again." You can. Maybe you can't change your situation — we can't always do that — and you have no way of knowing that any other situation would be better, it may be much worse.

Every moment of life is like God saying, "Look, I know you messed up the last moment, but here's a new one." Every moment you breathe, God's power envelops you and sustains you in existence. So every moment, no matter what you did in the last one, no matter if you were sinful, mean, impatient, unkind, or caustic, you have a fresh start in this new moment. Every day, every instant of your life is brand-new — you make it old by living in the past. And you make it a dream world by living in the future.

GOD'S WILL IN THE PRESENT MOMENT

We have to learn to live in the *Present Moment.* We have to ask God: What are You calling me to do now, in this Present Moment? Not yesterday or tomorrow, but right now. God's will is manifested to us in the duties and experiences of the Present Moment. We have only to accept them and try to be like Jesus in them.

ACTUAL GRACE IN THE PRESENT MOMENT

You know, when we look at God and we wonder why we are not closer to Him, and not like Jesus, we wonder why we were impatient yesterday and impatient today. We work so hard to overcome this weakness, this fault, and yet we don't do it. Then we keep praying: "Lord, give me patience," "Lord, give me love," "Lord, give me courage," "Give me endurance." "Give me, give me, give me." God gives, but you're not at home.

Every moment of life is new to you, and God gives you Actual Grace in that moment. It is different from Sanctifying Grace. If you are baptized and keeping the Commandments and loving your neighbor, then you are in a state of Sanctifying Grace. But God grants us the Actual Grace of this moment, not the grace of tonight or tomorrow, just the grace for *this moment.* So we mustn't project tomorrow into this moment, because God will not give us that grace now; He waits until it is needed.

I mean, I can say to myself that I would be a martyr for the faith if someone threatened my life and demanded that I renounce my Lord. I would hope I would have the courage to accept death, but you don't know what you would do because the trial is not here. God does not give me the grace today to endure the pain of tomorrow. But if I am living in the imagined pain of tomorrow with the grace I have now, I will always feel at a loss.

STARTING OVER

Very few people live in the Present Moment. It's like a new sheet of paper. Did you ever wish you could start all over again? Well, you can. That's what the Present Moment is. It's God giving you a brand-new sheet to begin again. But some people keep scribbling the same miserable thing on it.

THE DO/DROP SYSTEM

My "Do/Drop System" is to do it and drop it. When you live in the Present Moment you do whatever must be done, then you drop it and move on. You don't dwell on the past, or on your past accomplishments. That's all over. Do it and drop it.

DON'T LOOK BACK

Don't look back, because in order to look back you have to stop moving forward.

THE SHELF OF ILL MEMORIES

When you begin to feel angry, that feeling is stored on the shelf of your memory like a can of beans. And every now and then you take it down and swirl it around a little bit and taste it with your imagination, and you say to yourself, "I hate that person." Then you get tired of playing and you put it back on the shelf.

Every so often you take the can down once more. You do this over and over and over. And one day the can explodes, it spoils, and it does such damage to your soul. You are a mess spiritually, mentally, and at times physically. Forget the past or it will destroy your present.

LIMITS OUTSIDE THE PRESENT MOMENT

If I'm living in the future or I'm living in the past, I'm not receptive to the grace of the Present Moment. My mind is everywhere except in my own head, and then the imagination goes wild. You start limiting what you are capable of, based on past experience. You absolutely paralyze yourself.

55

You remember what Jesus said, "Sufficient for the day is the evil thereof" (Matt. 6:34)? All I have is today. And all of this takes tremendous self-control. It takes trust and practice.

GOD IS PRESENT

The Father in Heaven has an awesome attribute. The one I admire most is that everything is *now* for the Father; there is no past, no future with God; everything is now.

THE SACRAMENT OF THE PRESENT MOMENT

Mother Angelica first encountered the concept of the Present Moment while reading the work of Brother Lawrence when she was a young sister. The seventeenth-century lay Carmelite brother was crippled and in near constant pain following a brief career in the military. He wrote: "We need only to know God intimately present in us, to address ourselves to God at every moment . . . to practice the presence of God." Brother Lawrence believed that God could be worshipped anywhere by "making a chapel of the heart." These ideas coupled with those of Father Jean Pierre de Caussade would forever color the teachings and spirituality of Mother Angelica.

Brother Lawrence taught me about the Sacrament of the Present Moment. When I first read him, I realized I was getting too caught up in the problems of each day. They would overwhelm me. At that point, I decided I couldn't do that. You handle this moment, then the next, and then you forget about it and move on to the next moment. If you have to think of something in the future because it is part of the Present Moment, then you have to do that. But to bear everything that happened today and everything that will happen tomorrow all at one time is too much for anyone.

Our Lord taught: the past is dead, the future unborn, all that's mine is right now.

When we speak of the Sacrament of the Present Moment, what do we mean? First of all, a sacrament is an outward sign of an invisible reality. Let's look at the Eucharist and make a comparison. The Eucharist is, to the visible eye, a little wafer, a tiny, thin piece of flour and water. The Present Moment is also a very tiny, seemingly insignificant thing. But God is in both.

In Communion we receive His Body, Blood, Soul, and Divinity. In the Present Moment we receive the Will of God. If we accept His Will in the present moment, we have received God. The Will of God is always in the act of feeding you, transforming you, just as the Eucharist feeds you . . .

There is great similarity here. When we take the Eucharist, the host is consumed. When we accept the Will of God in the Present Moment, our will is consumed. The host is dissolved within me, and the Will of God dissolves my will. A perfect circle of union is established. Jesus gives Himself up for me in Communion, and in my daily life, I give myself up for Him. We mutually offer each other love for love. That's the Sacrament of the Present Moment.

What Can't Be Changed

What I can't change I put in God's hands, and that's that. It allows me to be unperturbed by the past.

No Limits

Whatever happens to me, I must personify Jesus at this moment, and then I have no limits on my love.

Difficult Present Moments

When the Present Moment comes and gives me something very difficult to bear, I say, "This is the will of God."

Think of when Pilate told the Lord,

"Don't you know I have the power to crucify you and the power to release you?" And Jesus said, "No, you would have no power over me if it had not been given to you from above" (John 19:10–11). Even at that awesome, unjust moment, Jesus saw the Father's Will and accepted it. In our daily lives we should too.

SERENE MOMENTS

One of the most calming effects upon our human nature is to live in the Present Moment. See, all I have to do is communicate and share with you whatever the Lord gives me right now. I don't have to worry about the next task, or the bills, I have to just concern myself with what I am doing *now.*

So the first thing you need to do to prepare your heart and your soul for prayer is to love God enough, to have the faith to see Him in the Present Moment; to have enough hope to know that God is going to bring good out of this moment no matter how bad it is; and to accept whatever the Present Moment brings you.

CLOSING THE DOOR

"When you pray, go to your private room, and when you have closed your door, pray to your Father . . ." (Matt. 6:6).

This "Closing the Door" that Our Lord is speaking about here is to live in the Present Moment. He is saying: close the door on yesterday, don't open it to tomorrow. Live here. Even in the Our Father, which follows this comment, He says, "Give us this day our daily bread" — meaning by the hour, by the moment. He is saying: "Close the door on your past no matter how bad it is." But most people cling to the past.

People who have lost their spouses six or seven years ago are still crying, still unhappy, living in the past. People with resentment so deep that it is like a growing cancer; day after day they add fuel to this terrible fire. Stop living in the past! Your husband did something ten, fifteen years ago, and you remind him of it at breakfast. How is that living in the Present Moment? Close the door on all that. Otherwise, you cannot pray an unceasing prayer, in which your heart, your soul is with God and you want to be like Jesus.

THE PRAYER OF THE PRESENT MOMENT

What a grace it is for God to call us to a higher spiritual plane. God wants you to be holy, to be for Himself. He wants you to have mental discipline, control, and serenity of soul. But how? There are various ways. You can always go to New York by way of California, which is what most people do in their prayer life. You can walk there, roller skate, or go by jet. The method I want to share with you is, I believe, the jet way. I have found it to be the most effective. Of all the methods of prayer, I have found this one to be the most powerful, the most cleansing, and the most peaceful. I call it the Prayer of the Present Moment.

Mental Discipline

Now what does living in the past or future have to do with prayer? As long as you are living there, you are not at home with God in this Present Moment. Your mind is so undisciplined that your doubts rule your life and you don't master your imagination, it masters you. I cannot arrive at any kind of prayer without mental discipline.

Now the Lord has asked us to "pray without ceasing." I cannot say prayers without ceasing, but I can sure pray without ceasing. If I have control over my past and future and live in this Present Moment, I am always available to God because my mind is clear and empty of *me*. St. Paul said that Our Dear Lord "emptied Himself" (Phil. 2:7). Well the essence of Christian living is to empty myself of me and to fill myself with Jesus. I've got to be empty of *me,* whether that me comes from the past or the future. I must have complete trust in God's mercy and providence. We must leave our entire past to His mercy and our whole future must rest in His providence. Most of us don't have that trust. But the more I love Jesus, the more I trust Him, the more I will seek Him out in this Present Moment. I cannot see God in the moment if I am not living in it.

How are you going to be able to see the Father's permitting will? To see God pruning you? Shaving off the rough corners? Leading you? I must be free of past and future attachments to have that vision. If I am in pain in this moment, I must see Him on His cross; in pain because of me. If I am insulted in this moment, I must see His humility, trying to make me humble. If I am experiencing joy in this moment, I must see His infinite mercy and goodness, which gives me something to laugh about. If I am successful in this moment I must thank Him.

You see, I must be at home with God; then my whole life becomes a prayer. I cannot speak with God if I have not "lived" a prayer all day! That's why so often when we go to prayer, we are distracted. You think about your husband, your children, your wife, your coworkers, Christmas gifts, the roast in the oven . . . by the time your prayer time ends, you're just calming your mind down. My friends, you cannot rise spiritually unless your whole day is a preparation for the moment when you and God speak together. You cannot rush in from the world and be filled with its concerns.

How to Find God in the Present Moment

No matter how much you learn about the spiritual life, the inevitable question arises: How? I know that I must rise from one level of prayer to another, and we know that dryness of soul is the pruning that God allows to promote us to a higher level. There is a difference between living in the Present Moment and concentrating on it. To live in the Present Moment takes love of Jesus. But how? What is the best way to live in this Present Moment, detached from the past and unconcerned about tomorrow — to live freely?

The best way I have discovered is meditation. Set aside some time for prayer. Meditate on something and you will find courage there. But then you will return to the activity of the day: that pile of dishes, the unruly children, the nagging wife, the nasty neighbor. It is very difficult to see Jesus in some people; particularly those who get on your nerves or are entrenched in deep sin. So we come to a dilemma.

Going constantly from a state of serenity with God to a state of chaos in the world creates a tension. Whether everything is ideal at home, which leads to lukewarmness, or you are enduring a cross, which can lead to despondency, the problem is the same: it is always difficult, in some way or other, to stay close to Jesus. In our meditation we must realize that this is *merely a springboard to a ceaseless kind of prayer* that is active.

We have a passive kind of prayer where we commune with God and He communes with us. (Don't be stingy with that part. If you can set aside an hour, give Him an hour.) Then we have an active prayer life. What is there in our prayer life that becomes active?

When we commune with God during prayer, we should never leave each other. Most of us leave Him there until we come back. It is a time totally separated from our day. There's a time for prayer, a time for work, a time for joy, a time for tears — you know we really work that to death. We forget that's in the Old Testament! We only have one time, and that's for Jesus.

So when you are alone with God, in this time of prayer, and you have shut everything out, you communicate. Then you and He go out together. This togetherness is not just Jesus and me, it is Jesus *in* me. "He who abides in me, and I in him, bears much fruit. For without me you can do nothing" (John 15:5).

Even after the "prayer time" has concluded, the meditation continues on because I must never lose sight of Jesus. If I recognize Him within my soul, I will see Him more easily in you. What I do to you, I do to Jesus. But my meditation is not geared to seeing Jesus; it is geared to being like Jesus. I empty myself and permit Jesus to act through me, and I know, through my meditation, how He would act in every situation. I absorb His gentleness, His mercy when I meditate on those instances where He practiced those virtues. Even thinking of the Holy Name of Jesus bears fruit; it has power. This meditation must bear fruit all day long. You must be what you were in your prayer time. Let Jesus trickle out throughout the day. Be merciful when you have an opportunity to judge, compassionate when you have an opportunity to be cold and indifferent. Unless you absorb Jesus during that time of meditation and give Him out as He is given to you, your prayer life is fruitless. We cannot have two facets of our lives — compartmentalized living. You must pray without ceasing and achieve a unity of life, a unity between your prayer and your actions. If you go with Jesus after meditation, together, He will bear fruit in you during each Present Moment, all day long.

A Summary

Your meditation should happen in the morning and should go with you throughout the day. The purpose of a meditation is to walk in the footsteps of Jesus so that as He was, you are — that is the heart of Christianity. We call it "putting on the mind of Christ," entering a new life. But the reason we do not consistently change is because we drop our prayer life and live an active life. We separate God from our daily existence. How am I going to see Jesus in this Present Moment? My human nature cannot do this unless I have Jesus, and realize that He is truly in my soul. If you saw Jesus standing right in front of you, how would you act? But He's closer than that. He's right in your heart. Why don't we act differently?

Your prayer life is twenty-four hours a day. You fill up at meditation in your prayer time when you are talking to Jesus, then you and Jesus go out into the world moment by moment. You don't live in yesterday and you don't live in tomorrow. You and He reenact His life. All of your life is a reenactment of His life.

Prayer for Healing the Memory

Heavenly Father, we put our weak selves before Your silent presence. You alone know the things forgotten and hidden that lie on the shelves of our memory. We cannot heal ourselves. We find it hard to forgive, and impossible to forget. Yet as we are absorbed and surrounded by Your Presence, we stand in that light and watch as the spiritual sores of us lepers disappear. The rotted limbs are restored, and our memories, at one time so ugly, are renewed and rejuvenated. Thank you, Lord. Amen.

4
EVERYDAY HOLINESS

A curious banner hung behind Mother Angelica whenever she spoke before crowds in the mid to late 1970s. In many ways, it described what would become her public mission for the next thirty years. The banner read: "Sounding the Call to Holiness."

Throughout her public life, Mother concerned herself with the sanctity of the common man. She sought to apply the timeless teachings of Christianity to the daily lives of people like her friends and relatives: the working-class Italians and African Americans she had known in her Canton, Ohio, youth. They were everyday, ordinary people. Common folk. She always said she was trying to reach "the man and woman in the pew," men and women like you and me. These were Mother's people and her primary focus.

Mother Angelica always felt that holiness had wrongly become the exclusive domain of religious and clergy. She believes we all have an obligation to strive for sanctity in very ordinary ways, at every moment.

CALLED TO HOLINESS

If you're breathing and you've got two legs, you're called to holiness.

EVERYDAY HOLINESS

I want you to have a new concept of holiness. You've got to be holy where you are: washing the dishes, at the office, at school. Wherever you are, you can be holy there.

A SCHOOL OF HOLINESS

All life is a school of holiness and everything that happens to you from bad weather to an ingrown toenail is an opportunity for you to be like Jesus. Don't miss the opportunity.

LIVING HOLINESS

We need to look at holiness today in the light of living it, not knowing about it. Christians need to do more than think about their faith; they have to exemplify it.

BELIEVERS?

The early Christians were simply called "believers" because their life bore the fruit of their beliefs. How are you to tell a Christian from a pagan? Joy, peace, gentleness, patience. Well, if you are as impatient and combustible, as mean, hateful, and unkind as your pagan neighbor, what is this "believing"? Or is it unbelieving?

CONFINED FAITH

I find people have faith coming out of their ears, and that's as far as it goes: above their shoulders. It has never entered their heart enough to change them.

WILLINGNESS TO CHANGE

A woman was dragged by a friend to the monastery one afternoon. I met her and offered her a set of my mini books on the spiritual life. She declined. I said, "Why don't you want to take them with you?" She said, "Because I don't want to change." Boy, I thought, this woman is bad off. We must be constantly willing to change into what the Father wants us to be. What you want is unimportant. After all, what do you know?

THE EYES OF GOD

You have got to learn to look at events, at everything that happens, through the eyes of God and not your own selfishness.

When God Speaks

God speaks to us often. Through parents, friends, relatives, conditions, circumstances, and everything that happens to us. Every moment of the day He is speaking to us, and many times He encourages us to do good things for our neighbor, for the Kingdom. And we're willing to do them under certain conditions (since we always put conditions on God). God wants us to do great things for Him, and the greatest thing of all is our own holiness.

Where You Are

The third chapter of Colossians says, "You're God's chosen race. You're His saints. He loves you." Well, now you've got to act like one, which means to act very human. Holiness begins wherever you are.

It doesn't take a lot to be holy; only thought and a little perseverance.

Holiness

Holiness is a beautiful struggle.

What Holds Us Back?

We've got to figure out what those first Christians had that we lack today. What is it that smothered real Christianity in our hearts?

What is it in your life and in my life that smothers the real truth? What is covering it over? Is it riches? Is it a desire for human glory? Is it lust? Is it alcohol? Is it sex? Pride? What is it that covers up the glory of the kingdom and makes us desire the very least? Why are we willing to spend eternity in a mud shack, when we could have a spiritual mansion?

Brilliance Is Not Required

Every time Jesus taught the multitudes, the apostles would get Him alone afterward and say, "Master, would you explain the parable to us?" Every child in that audience knew exactly what He was talking about, except his apostles.

Now some of you look at Scripture and you don't understand it. Then someone comes along with an insight that makes you feel teeny-tiny. Well don't! You aren't alone. Holiness doesn't consist of knowing much, or doing much, but of loving much.

A New Awareness

A Christian does not strain after God the way one seeks a lost object, he merely becomes more and more aware of what he already possesses.

WE MAKE OR BREAK US

If it wasn't for people, we could all be holy. But it really isn't other people who make or break us. We are the ones who make or break us.

FORGIVENESS AND HOLINESS

Being holy isn't hard. You've got a thousand opportunities every day. Do you remember what St. Paul says in Colossians? Now, remember this man had a violent quarrel with Barnabas to the point where they parted company. He says in chapter 3, verse 13: "Bear with one another; forgive each other as soon as a quarrel begins." This man learned that by hard experience. It didn't come easy for Paul. It's not going to come easy for you either. But the next time someone wrongs you, forgive them quickly. Begin in your heart. And remember, it's merely an opportunity for holiness.

THE CHRISTIAN WITNESS

The witness of a Christian is holding your temper when you want to choke somebody. It's being nice to your wife when she looks like an old rag in the morning and burns your toast — again! The witness demonstrates that there's something more important than toast. We are called to bear fruit. And the fruit is *your life.* The witness is something alive inside of you, not your words. It's showing the world that you can face the trials of everyday life with love and compassion.

LISTENING YOUR WAY TO HOLINESS

Some people are always complaining. Every time you talk to them you get an organ recital. It begins with their liver, then it moves on to the stomach, the heart, plantar warts, dandruff. Who knew there were so many organs?

You know what holiness is? Listening to all that as if you had never heard it before. Holiness is listening to that joke you've heard twenty-five times and laughing at the punch line for the twenty-sixth time, while keeping your mouth shut. Holiness is putting up with the gripes of others with tenderness. All of that is holiness.

THE STRUGGLE

I don't want any of you to ever think that you are not going to have a struggle. Holiness is a constant struggle. It is not something you arrive at and enjoy while the rest of humanity wallows in imperfections. We are an imperfect, miserable bunch of people — and we're gonna be that way until we die. Sinners? Let's hope not. Imperfect? You bet.

You're going to have inclinations, temptations to anger, lust, gluttony. Don't blame it all on the devil. You have a lot to do with it too, sweetheart. I think the old guy gets more credit than he deserves. So examine your own heart and keep struggling to make the right choices.

HOLINESS COMES SLOWLY

St. Paul, the same man who had a violent argument with Barnabas, said, "Love is patient, love is kind" (1 Cor. 13:4). He got to that point, growing one step at a time.

Sometimes in a family we don't give each other enough time to grow. You don't become a saint overnight. The growth is constant and often slow.

FAITH AND ITS FRUITS

Faith is a gift given to us at baptism that enables us to accept invisible realities. For instance if someone says, "How do you know there is a heaven? Do you know anyone who has been there?" Well, you can't answer that. So you say "I believe." There is something within you that gives you that certainty, that assurance. It's a gift.

Today, many think that faith is something within their power. It sends me up a wall when people say, "If you had more faith you could be healed." What is this faith business in their minds? Some kind of magic formula?

How do you get more faith? Not by presumption. You're dealing with God. Our petulant demands are not faith, and we are not omnipotent. Making demands on God is not faith, that's a subtle kind of pride. God is not your personal slot machine! Faith breeds a humility that is willing to accept the truth that the Father has revealed to us through His Son Jesus, knowledge that Christ is the Lord, and a deep realization that within the soul dwells the Spirit. When you believe these things about Jesus and know that it comes from His Father, it must bear the fruit of faith.

Most people possess the gift of faith, but they don't bear the fruit of that faith. The fruit of faith is to change your life. If you believe Jesus came to save you and give you an example of how to live, then you must live like Him. That's the fruit of faith.

Unreasonable?

Faith is not unreasonable. We are unreasonable.

Sleepy Little Sanctifications

For Mother Angelica nothing is beyond sanctification or the reach of grace. In her personal life, she makes brief offerings to God throughout the day. These "little oblations" can be easily mimicked and help to lace the day with acts of faith. Even sleep should not be overlooked . . .

One-third of your life is spent sleeping. If you are sixty, that's twenty years! But do we give our sleep to the Lord before retiring each night? We should say, "Lord, I unite my sleep tonight to Your sleep: when You were a Babe, when You were grown and tired. I unite it with the nightly rest of the Blessed Mother."

All of a sudden, there I am snoozing along — but it's sanctified. I've made my sleep holy.

Uniting Every Day to God

Everything I do today is united to God. If I want to be like Jesus, I have to start uniting even the mundane things in my life to Him.

I have an EWTN vice president's meeting at ten o'clock. So how am I going to unite that to God? Well, I'm sure Our Lord had many, many meetings with His apostles. He says several times in the Gospel, "Let's go aside and be alone." He must have met them in a house, maybe Peter's house, to plan their next journey. So I can unite this meeting, which is sometimes rather boring, to Our Lord counseling and meeting with the apostles. That way something that may be a pain in the neck, once in a while, becomes holy.

Suppertime Holiness

It's people that bug you, did you ever notice that? Take some of you wives. The husband's gone, the kids are gone, and you exhale, you breathe again. Maybe they're breathing too! And you have your whole day planned: you're going to throw your laundry in and watch one of those stupid soap operas where everybody is always living with everybody else. Someone's always on trial, lost, or kidnapped. Suddenly you hear this bang in the basement and there is water all over the floor. While you were cleaning that up, the roast burned. Then the school called to tell you that Johnny fell and broke his arm — "Please come pick him up." Then you trudge in, just as your husband is arriving home from work. He puts his briefcase down and announces, "Boy, you gals got it easy."

That's when you can do one of two things: sock him or love him — knowing that he too has had a hard day. You see, we endure each other rather than living with each other. We are always looking at what's wrong with ourselves, other people, and the world. You have to understand that human relationships make for holiness, not hell, because they give us an opportunity to act like Jesus and love under various circumstances.

HOLINESS, NOT PERFECTION

When you look at the Present Moment you must make a choice to be like Jesus. Even if you don't make it, if you've blown your stack, you can gain more merit by being humble over it. See, you can't lose.

Don't let anything pull you back. You are a holy people that God came and died for and gave grace to. He is not asking you to be a perfect people; *He is asking you to be*

79

you, choosing to be Him in the Present Moment. God wants you to love your neighbor as he is struggling to be holy.

A Scheduled Life Is a Holy Life

We've got to rediscover the limits of "work time." In monastic life everything is scheduled. One of the sacrifices of religious life is that you're never really able to finish anything. Work time is set for a few hours, and after that it's prayer time, meal time, and so on. The problem with businesspeople, and especially CEOs, is they run themselves ragged getting stuck in "work time."

I never did think that anyone should be obsessed by their work. I don't think they're busy. I think that if you've made it to CEO you ought to have, by that point, the time you need to keep your family together and keep your soul fed. If you've gotten that far, you shouldn't still be in the middle of the rat race or you're not very smart. You've got to measure your time, and that time you measure out belongs to one purpose alone.

If you look at the Scriptures, you'll find that the Lord got up early in the morning while the apostles were still sleeping. He'd go up on a mountain and He would be alone with His Father for hours before the apostles woke. That was His time with His

80

Father. Then when the apostles got up, it was His time with the community, of which He was the head. Then when the sun rose and the people began to appear, it was His time with the people. I followed that pattern and I think it works. It will work for others too.

You do what God wants you to do, but you've got to drop it when He calls you to the next thing. I think every father, mother, boss, and worker has to do this. The man cannot bring the troubles of home to the office with him. Similarly, when he walks through the door of his home he has to be a father, a husband. And if he carries everything with him it's a total disaster. Otherwise you're not present for anything or anybody. You're always in a state of confusion. You're always in a hurry and focused on something else. There is an advantage to having a minor monastic spirit in the world, one that forces you to ask yourself: Am I possessing what I am doing, or is it possessing me?

THE LACK OF SILENCE

Today everything is noise. You call to order something and you've got to listen to bebop music while you're waiting for the salesperson. You go to the dentist and he's got more music. Like that's going to help when he comes at you with the drill . . . I suppose you would say, "Well, I would rather have that than silence in the dental chair." I don't know. Maybe you'd have time to pray. But everywhere we go there has to be something to block our thought patterns. And what does it do? Many times it takes us away from God, just when we need Him most.

SAYING YES TO GOD

To be able to say yes to God at every moment of our lives is the essence of holiness. It really doesn't matter whether you are at prayer, whether you are working, whether you're recreating, whether you're eating or sleeping — nothing should separate you from Jesus.

HOLY WORK

Every work can be a holy work. Look at laundry for a minute. We are all in the cleansing business. Just like I cleanse my soul, I can use this mundane type of work to remind me that I am a work of purification. I can offer the laundry to God so that the clothes I wash are not only purified from dirt, but they may purify the soul who wears them or uses them.

WHERE YOUR MIND SHOULD BE

Don't allow your mind to be in the world. Your body is here, but your mind should be with the Lord, as if nothing else mattered.

KEEPING THE FACETS SHARP

I have a crystal rosary that my mother gave me. She used it for many years. It's dull because all the facets that make crystal sparkle are worn away. You can clean or wash it, but whatever made it attract light is gone. Well, you can't let that happen in your soul. The facets of our heart must always be sharp, clear, and pointed toward God.

SEEK FIRST THE KINGDOM

Never permit your soul to desire anything but God and His Glory. Self-seeking disrupts the soul and places it in a state of confusion. Seek first His kingdom, and you will find heaven within.

SEEING HOLINESS

It is very important for your neighbor to *see* the fruit of your holiness of life, the fruit of God living in you. St. Paul says, "The Spirit of God has made His home in you" (Rom. 8:9). The Spirit of the Lord within you is so overwhelming that it should be the most important and visible thing in your entire life.

CHOOSING GOD

You know there are many dilemmas in Christianity, many paradoxes. For example, the Lord said to honor your mother and father. But then He said: "If any man comes to me without hating his mother, father, wife, children, brothers, sisters, yes and his own life too, he cannot be my disciple" (Luke 14:26). Which sounds like a contradiction, but it's not. It means that I should honor and love those most close to me: my blood relations, my family, and my friends. But if it came time to choose between them — my possessions, all the things I love — and God, I must go with God.

He didn't say we couldn't love anything; He just said, prefer Me to everything. If you lost all the things in your life, all the people in your life, you would still have that supernatural peace of mind.

TRANQUILITY AND THE LORD

The difference between the peace that a Buddhist acquires and a Christian acquires is love for Christ. When I see a statue of Buddha, the image of tranquility, I always

84

want to go scratch his big, fat tummy. You see, that kind of tranquility is only based on the control of oneself in regard to nothing. But self-control for a Christian is the possession of one's mind, one's soul, by God. I have chosen a Lord.

Scripture says, "If your lips confess that Jesus is Lord and if you believe in your heart that God raised him from the dead, then you will be saved" (Rom. 10:9). Some have cut it short and say, "Whoever believes in Jesus is saved." No. The devil believes in Jesus, but he is not saved. It's "Jesus is Lord" that makes you saved. He must be the Lord of your life.

SPIRITUAL GROWTH AND LOVE

Unless we continue to transform ourselves to the image of Jesus, we remain spiritual children. As Scripture says, "Jesus advanced in wisdom, and age, and grace before God and men" (Luke 2:40). Many Christians today are, spiritually, about twelve years old. They shoot up prayers to the big Father and they know somehow that He will answer them. This is the level of growth that they have achieved.

You were not created to be a complacent bump on a log. Not in this life. What you want to do is advance in holiness. And you advance in proportion to how long it takes you to say yes to God, and love the neighbor you like the least. Love is to wish well, to do well, and to pray for another. On that level, you can love anybody.

Love Is . . .

Love is not a feeling. It is a decision. Jesus cannot command that you have a feeling. He can only command us to make a decision, and love is the greatest decision we will ever make.

Transforming Union

When the love of God and your love are the same, we call that Transforming Union. The Eternal Word, Jesus in you, must always respond to the Father in your neighbor. This is how you build the Holy Spirit.

Seek the Beloved

Like the bride in the canticle, you have to seek the Beloved. And though He peeks between the lattices, going this way and that, you see just parts of His face. He's there. He's always there. He is so terribly in love with you that He cannot leave you. You leave Him.

The Little Flower said, "People have a

hard time accepting the love of God." What did the Lord say? "I don't want one sacrifice, I want your heart, my love."

We Become What We Love

We have the wrong idea of Christianity. We don't understand that to know Jesus is to want to be like Him.

Do you notice that after people reach fifty years of married life they put their pictures in the paper and they look alike? Love does this. Love makes you like the person you love. If you really loved Jesus, you would look more and more like Him each day.

Christianity

Do you know what Christianity is? It's blood and guts. Christianity is Someone that you're in love with: Jesus the Lord. And when you're in love with Jesus, you're going to love your wife more, you're going to love your husband more, you're going to love your children more, because only the love of Jesus can make you love deeply, truly.

That Kid of Mine

The greatest evils today are fear and lukewarmness. Jesus said, "I wish you were hot or cold, but you are lukewarm and I will vomit you from my mouth" (Rev. 3:15–16). We have a fantastic amount of lukewarmness in the world today, because we don't see Jesus in the Present Moment. Every moment you are meeting Jesus face to face.

Some woman told me the other day, "Are you telling me that mean kid of mine is Jesus?" Yes, hidden in that kid is Jesus. It is your duty to bring Him out with love, patience, and compassion.

A STOMACH FOR FAITH

Don't be afraid to be frustrated. Look at me, I take a lot of Maalox. Somebody said to me not long ago, "I'm surprised that a woman of such great faith would have to take Maalox." I said, "My friend, my stomach doesn't know about my great faith."

THE LOOK OF HOLINESS

Holiness to most people is looking holy. They think a holy person is one who never loses his temper. Oh please! They think a holy person never feels impatient. Well, there is not an Italian born who is patient, and since there are more Italian saints than any other nationality, there must be something about being impatient that makes you holy.

Fear and Faith

I remember when I had a spinal operation and the doctors told me I might never walk again. I was scared. I shook in that bed and I was petrified, but I said, "Lord, I know You'll take care of me." And believe me, I shook all the way to the operating room. The Lord did take care, but not before I had to go through a real purification period. I had to believe when I saw nothing, and seeing nothing is scary. So don't feel bad if you have a similar reaction — if you feel afraid and you question. Don't think for a minute it is because you lack faith. Sometimes all that fear is the road to faith.

Faith in Distress

Faith seeks the God of consolations more than the consolations of God.

The Crucifix

You know I wear a crucifix because I don't want to forget that God is with me. I like to hold on to Him when things get difficult, because it reminds me how much Jesus loves me. He loved me this much. He wants me to understand that in this position, in this intolerable, painful position, He forgave. That's what it means to be saintly.

Arrows of Love

We miss millions of tiny opportunities to be one with God during the day. We get something in our heads and it goes round and round; and first thing you know, half the day is gone, and you haven't been with the Lord.

All you have to do is find some commonality between what you are doing and what Jesus did. For instance, if you are traveling and fatigued, frustrated from running from one gate to another, ask yourself: "How many times did Our Lord make a journey without sleep? How tired His legs must have been walking miles and miles wearing sandals." See, you can create these little arrows of love, these points of commonality between yourself and the Lord before work, during work, or after work. It's so simple, but very powerful.

Holiness Is Light

Holiness is not a match light or a 50-watt bulb, it's a supernova — one holy person can save a city, a nation.

Evangelization

The essence of evangelization is to tell everybody, "Jesus loves you." In this society people are suffering and in despair. If we don't tell them about Jesus they have nowhere to go.

PROCLAIMING THE GOOD NEWS WHERE YOU ARE

Don't complain about the Church. You are the Church, and God has destined you to proclaim the Good News by example, by family life, by holy single life, by faithfulness. He wants you to be holy wherever you are. The simple duties of your life, done with love, cause great rejoicing in the entire kingdom.

WHOLLY SATISFIED

Our Lord said, "Blessed are those who hunger and thirst for holiness, they shall be satisfied" (Matt. 5:6). Today what is holiness? Holiness is that image of Jesus in your heart that shines on your face and tells your neighbor that there is more to come, and it's better than this life. It makes you so free that you can laugh at the world and what it has to offer. Others look at you and ask, "What do you have? I want it."

TRUE FREEDOM

Jesus came and gave us Good News. Not only has he redeemed us, given us part of his nature in Baptism, but He has also made us children of God. As a child of God, I am free; meaning that no matter what life dishes out, I can overcome it. Because it will be Jesus in me overcoming those challenges. The Good News calls us to let Jesus take over so it isn't as difficult anymore.

5
God's Will and Providence

One finds a radical devotion to God's Will throughout Mother Angelica's life and teaching. She entrusted not only her person, but her community, and later her network to the Will of God. Each day she submitted all of her pursuits to His Providence, confidently believing that God would provide all that was necessary in His good time. He came through, and then some.

Below is her advice for all who desire to know God's Will in their lives, who wish to live in His Providence, and who hope to achieve greater union with the Almighty.

God's Will

"What is God's Will for me?" Somebody asked me that not too long ago. Honey, if it's happening, it's God's Will; and you have to correspond to it in the Present Moment. God's Will in the moment is like a sacrament.

A Broom for God

You must strive to have your will in such union with God's that you want nothing else. You don't care what happens. That's real humility. Be like a broom in a corner. If the Master comes in, sweeps the floor a bit, puts it in the corner, lets it fall on the floor, puts it on the highest shelf, it should make no difference to you. Be a broom for God. Let Him brush you around, push you about. Do what He wants.

Get Out of the Way

I've learned that when you deal with God, get out of the way! I think that's the best advice I could offer you. Because He has plans that we wouldn't think of in a million years. You need to just let God do whatever He wants to do; and watch what happens.

The Simplicity of Holiness

Holiness it simple. Holiness is doing God's Will in the Present Moment. That's it. Holiness consists of four words: the Will of God.

Feelings

It doesn't matter how you feel, it only matters what you do. Our Lord Himself said that when He told the story of the man who had two sons whom he asked to go into the vineyard. One said no, but he went. The other son said yes, and never went. Who did the father's will? The one who said he didn't feel like going, but went anyway (Matt. 21:28–31). That's the example we must follow.

GOD'S WILL IN YOUR LIFE

People often ask me, "How do you know whether something is God's Will in your life?" I say, "Ask me next year, and then we'll know whether it was God's Will."

The Lord isn't going to come down and say, "Now, look sweetie, I want you to do this little thing for me." He's not going to do that. He gave you a brain. He gave you a memory, an intellect, a will. Do you realize if you're a Christian, you have Sanctifying Grace in you? The Holy Spirit is *in* you. Pray. Move forward in His grace, and you will discover His Will for you.

DISCERNING GOD'S WILL FOR YOU

A problem many of us face is discerning exactly what God's Will is for us in a particular circumstance. When confronted with a tough decision or an unexpected choice, we often don't know what to do. For fellow sufferers,

Mother offers some relief.

How do you evaluate God's Will in your life? I don't think God's Will always makes you feel good. You judge God's Will as follows:

1. Does it violate any of the Commandments? Is it against the precepts of the Church?
2. Will it give God honor and glory?
3. Will it benefit my family and my spiritual life?

That is how you can judge what God's Will is for you. And sometimes we don't have clarity even with that. I would pray more at that point. I would ask Our Lord to give you light. If somehow along the way we miss it, He will make good out of your mistakes. You can depend on that.

PERFECT JOY IN THE WILL OF GOD

Brother Leo once asked our holy father, St. Francis, "Father, in what lies pure joy?"

St. Francis said, "Well, I'll tell you. When we go to the monastery, if the monk comes out, doesn't recognize us and slams the door in our face, and we rap again and he yells at us, 'Thieves, robbers be gone!' slamming the door once more; if we are out in the cold and the snow and when we rap again the monk comes out and throttles us, therein lies perfect joy."

"That's perfect joy?" Brother Leo said.

"It is," St. Francis replied. "If we can take that for the sake of Jesus, and be joyful with it all, therein lies perfect joy."

What does this little anecdote mean? It means that happiness is not always ours. It is very short-lived sometimes. We all know that. But joy is forever. "Your hearts will be full of joy," the Lord tells us, "and that joy no one shall take from you" (John 16:22). See, joy is the acceptance of God's Will, whether it is a crust of bread or a fresh loaf, whether it is being throttled in the snow, or sitting before a warm fire. If God allows it, or admits it, or ordains it, what's the difference? It's there.

In the acceptance of whatever happens, lies perfect joy.

No Excuses

We are in the habit today of making excuses. And because our faith is very low and weak, we can excuse ourselves from answering God's call, from doing God's Will, from listening to the Church, from listening to the Gospel.

Look at St. Paul in Second Corinthians and you'll find that there is a man who had an excuse not to be a real Christian. He talks about being shipwrecked, beaten, in danger of rivers, in danger of robbers, in danger of open country. The man had all kinds of excuses not to be a Christian, not to continue, not to persevere. But we must put aside the excuses and realize that God works with failure and brokenness.

ANGELICA'S MOTTO

Jesus is my strength. Jesus is my rock. I trust His wisdom and His Will in my life.

OBEDIENCE OF WILL

We are all bound by obedience. We are bound by obedience because the striking characteristic of the Lord is His total obedience. Our lady is no different. Religious are bound to their vows. Married people are bound by their marriage vows to each other. We must all submit our wills to the Will of God. The most serious problem we have is an attachment to our own will.

How am I going to be holy? By detaching myself from my will. That's why Our Dear Lord said to the apostles, "My food is to do the will of the One who sent me" (John

4:34). That sentence should be ours as much as it was the Lord's. But if we feed ourselves constantly with our will, with our own pleasure, with what we want, then holiness will elude us.

You may feel better for a while, but your will, eventually, becomes a slave driver. It's the will that takes us to heaven, purgatory, or the lower region. That's what the devil is after, and once you give your will over to Satan, you're miserable, and he'll throw you down as soon as he can — as soon as he has served his purpose. Why does he push man to sex, to lust, to drugs, to alcohol? Because it weakens the will. You have no self-control. Why does he entice you to do your own will? Because that's what Satan did. He defied God and did his own thing.

AVOIDING GOD'S WILL

What is it in your life that makes you run once you begin to feel that God is after you? I'll tell you why you run, because you're afraid He's going to take everything away from you that's dear. There's a beautiful line in a poem by Frances Thompson and it says, "What I took from thee, I took not for thy harm, but only that you would seek it in My arms." Remember that! Don't ever be afraid to follow Jesus, to be a real Christian on fire with what you believe.

WHY I'M HERE

I'm not here to win friends and influence people. I'm here to do God's Will. Now, if the accomplishment of that will bugs a lot of people, well, that's their problem. I can't help that.

GOD'S PENANCE

Penance doesn't mean a thing if it's not God's Will. St. Teresa of Avila was so determined that she was going to do all these penances one Lent. Well, she got into bed and was so sick everybody had to wait on her. She complained to the Lord, and He said to her: "That was your penance, but this is mine for you."

We all have ideas of how we're going to be holy and how we're going to do penance. It's amazing what we'll do if it's our will, but if it's God's Will we all scream.

"IT'S MY LOVE"

When I was a young nun, I had a pretty rough time. I was always sick with something, and there were sisters who just drove me up the wall. I was at adoration one night in the chapel and I knelt down and looked up at the Blessed Sacrament and said, "Why does all this stuff have to happen to me? I'm trying so hard and nothing works — nothing. Then I went to my abbess and she keeps saying, 'It's God's Will.' Why does it always have to be Your will to treat us so miserably?"

When I finally calmed down I heard this very gentle voice. "Try saying, 'It's My love,' " He said. God has mercy on drunks, children, and nuns who are not very bright. I learned the hard way that everything that happens is His love, because His love and His Will are one and the same.

GOD'S LOVE/GOD'S WILL

Do you really believe God loves you? If you do, you know everything that happens in your life is for your good. And it isn't always a peaceful experience.

UNION WITH GOD

The following excerpt was found among the notes of Sister Mary Raphael, who became Angelica's spiritual daughter in the early 1950s. This quote is one of the earliest teachings of Mother Angelica and probably dates from the mid-fifties or early sixties. It captures one of Mother's favorite lessons, one she never tired of conveying to her sisters.

We are anxious and troubled over many things, consequently our faith becomes weak and we lose sight of the fact that we can become saints, not because of what we are, but because of what He is and what He can make of us. Love is the one thing necessary. You must love God with your whole mind, your whole heart, with all your strength. He must be your all . . .

How much fuller your life would be if the Lord had a more personal part in it. Ask Him to go to work with you. Seek His advice and help in anything difficult. In short, let Him be your Constant Companion throughout the day. Let Him see with your eyes, hear with your ears, work with your hands, give peace through your goodwill, and most importantly, let Him love with your heart. This loving union is for simple souls and will, if faithfully practiced, lead to great heights of sanctity. Did not Jesus say, "I am the way" (John 14:6)? Then He will teach you this life of loving union. Remember, it is the love you put into each act of uniting yourself to Jesus that counts.

Let your joy find its fulfillment in God's work in you, at every moment. Fall in love with His Will.

Prayer for Greater Union with God
There's a prayer I love:

Christ be under me. Christ be over me. Christ be beside me, on the left of me, on the right of me. This day be within and without me. Christ the lowly and meek, all powerful, be in the heart of each to whom I speak, in the mouth of each who speaks to me, in all who draw near me or see me or hear me. Amen.

That's union with God.

Prayer for Union with God's Will

Pour within us Father that compassion, that mercy that comes from Thee. Lord Jesus, allow us to image you as you image the Father.

May we see Your Will in everyone and everything, and in all circumstances. Like children, make us meek and humble of heart. We ask that you imprint Your own Spirit upon us. Indelibly sign us with Thine own Will so that Thy Will and our wills may be one. We ask this in the name of Jesus. Amen.

GOD'S PROVIDENCE

God loves me so much that He provides for my every need. God's providence disposes and directs everything for His honor and glory, and for the good of my soul. I must consider all of God's creation from a very personal perspective. Look how the sun contributes to my well-being. It melts the snow to swell the rivers, and draws the water up again to rain upon the fields, nourishing the corn that I eat. It hardens the clay to make dishes for me to eat upon. We have lost our sense of awe in God's creation and that is a pity.

From the largest galaxy to the minutest bacteria in a drop of water, God has willed it all. Everything that God created was created for a reason, and if this is true of things, how much more is it true of you and of me. So I must remember that every situation in my life is permitted by God for my good. You know, His providence is so immense and powerful. Though it embraces all of creation, it takes care of every tiny detail of my life. The Lord said the very hairs of my head are numbered . . .

His providence surrounds me like a cloak. I neither live nor move without it. He keeps the entire universe in order, and still finds time to take a personal interest in you and me.

THE STAMP OF PROVIDENCE

In daily events I must see the providence of God. Remember this one little truth: Nothing happens to you without the stamp of His providence placed upon it before it happens. That's faith.

YES OR NO

Faith is seeing God's providence when He says yes and seeing His love when He says no. You see, it takes a lot of love on the part of God to say no to you. Why? Because He risks your love; He risks your faith in Him; He risks your hope in Him. If you are asking for something and it isn't for your good, His love will say no. But if you are asking for something that will bring about good, His providence moves events in your favor, and the Lord allows it.

SEE IT NOW

His providence extends to even the suffering in your life, to even the most painful moments. He weighs every sorrow in your life in the scale of His mercy. He fits the cross to your shoulder. He knows just what cross you can carry the best. His providential action is present in every human event. You may not understand it now, but you will later on.

If you look back in your life, you will find many times things happened that were so disappointing — yet as you look back you can see the good and the reason for their happening. Why can't you see it now? Why must we have twenty-twenty vision only in hindsight? Why can't we trust His providence today?

WHY DOES GOD PERMIT EVIL?

Why does God permit evil? Perhaps this is our stumbling block. His providence protects the freedom of His creatures by permitting evil. If you reject God and turn against Him with your free will, God will still draw good out of it — for your good or for the good of another.

He gives us opportunities to rise after a fall with humility and added strength, knowing that He will provide for me in the future. His providence helps me to choose the right thing at the right time. But — it's so wonderful — if I make the wrong choice, His providence still stands by me. The Father disposes and directs everything for my good.

God knows your every need and desire. He listens to your every sigh and sees every tear. He surrounds you completely. Even though you do not see the end of the road, you need not fear.

LUCK?

We ascribe everything wonderful to luck. What is luck? There is no such thing as luck. God is the author. He is the prime mover of everything that is — even your heartbeat, your breath. And we never think of those things.

Our religious order is dedicated to thanksgiving. We thank God for all these wondrous things, but we thank Him for those who might never thank Him, those who attribute everything to their own intelligence and their own talents. God sustains us all, so anything that is good or fruitful comes from God, not from us. The Lord could take it all away from you tomorrow, and you would be a babbling idiot. We depend on Him every moment of our lives. It's a wonderful feeling of confidence that comes into our hearts when we realize that we depend on Jesus for everything.

SPIRITUAL INVINCIBILITY

A soul that trusts God is invincible.

GOD'S PROVIDENCE IS EVER MOVING

God's Will is never inactive. It is only inactive to you, because you cannot see further than your nose. God's providence is ever working and bearing fruit. When you pray, God has heard it. When the Lord refuses you, or nothing seems to be happening, something is happening. We may see no solution to our problems and no relief in sight, but faith is always there to assure us that in the end, we will triumph.

Prayer of Abandonment to Divine Providence

O merciful Father, Your providence surrounds and protects me with loving concern. Grant me the humility to give myself totally to Your care with peace. Amen.

6
LIVING PRAYER AND TRUE SPIRITUALITY

Aside from communal prayer, Mother Angelica spent several hours in private meditation each day. This contemplative prayer, usually in her monastery chapel, was the foundation of Mother's day and the impetus for all she would achieve. But her prayer wasn't confined to the chapel. Mother Angelica developed a method of prayer that could be practiced amid the activities of her workday. Being a full-time abbess and the CEO of a major cable network demanded a fresh spiritual approach, and Mother discovered one. She shares it below, as well as her thoughts on prayer and a few practical applications for your spiritual life.

PRAYER

Prayer is to take your failings, your evil tendencies and struggle with them.

Prayer prepares you to get rid of all those things inside yourself that are not like Jesus.

Prayer creates a disposition of assurance

— not that you're going to get every answer that you want — but assurance of God's presence and His love.

Prayer to Someone

When you start to think of prayer as Someone, you are finally about to speak to God.

True Prayer

A lot of people today pray, but they never talk to God. Why don't you speak up and really talk to God, heart to heart, like a friend? You say a lot of things to friends.

Some of you are great sinners who never speak to God. I'll bet His ears will really open up when He hears that strange voice coming from below. Don't wait for something to happen. Talk to Him about everyday things right now.

More Than "Gimme"

God wants to hear us, but He wants to hear something more than "Gimme." You never talk over with God what He wants. It's always what you want. Did you ever think there are other things in the world that are just as important, or more important, than you are? Have you ever prayed for your neighbor next door, your city, your country?

A Release of Love

Prayer is the release of our love with assurance that we are loved in return.

Prayer is your heartbeat in rhythm with His.

Pray as you love.

The Challenge of Christianity

We are trying to arrive at a degree of prayer that is applicable to your daily life. We make excuses for ourselves, claiming that high degrees of prayer are for people who aren't married, for nuns. Well that's not true. Jesus died for all of us, and He wants us all to be holy. This is the challenge of Christianity. So let's knock all our self-imposed excuses out. We just don't want to make the effort. Holiness is for everyone.

Silence for God

Silence is not something that you can impose from the outside in. It's something that's inside and it must grow and be concentrated. Without it you cannot achieve holiness, because you cannot hear God and neither can you speak to Him.

If you are so busy with the noise of the world, with the noise of events, with the noise of things around you — yourself, your work, your friends — even when it is extremely quiet, you can't hear anything. Your powers of concentration are so diverted that you cannot concentrate on God.

The Soul

An event in your soul is like an event in the depths of the ocean. It's very deep. On the ocean there may be turmoil, a storm, or a gentle breeze. But the further you go down, there is absolute, total silence. And that's the way it is with the soul.

The soul lives in silence. You have to feel that silent place in the depths of your soul, in that place where you can always concentrate on God. It's a place nobody can go and nothing can enter, unless you open the door.

Living Prayer

Prayer is food for the soul. We go through an awful lot to eat. The other day the sisters spent two or three hours preparing dinner, and it took us about fifteen minutes to annihilate it.

Some people pray like they eat breakfast, dinner, and supper. It's about a fifteen-minute experience. Some pray in the morning as an exclamation of distress: "God help me today." That's their morning prayer. At noon they look at God and say: "Well, you didn't do much this morning, maybe you can do better this afternoon." And in the evening, they are so disgusted and disgruntled that they say, "I had faith, but you didn't come through."

There is a better way. Jesus calls us to pray without ceasing. The Unceasing Prayer is purifying. It allows you to turn your entire life into a living prayer. It is the type of prayer that makes you grow in holiness. Now, most of us are very confused by the Unceasing Prayer because we think we must pray constantly all day. But in reality it has nothing to do with saying prayers. *Because prayer is not something, it is someone and that someone is Jesus.*

If you love someone, a husband or a wife, and you know that something would please them very much, like, say, a table; you begin to work on it in secret. Throughout the building process your mind is on the table. You notice every detail and you adjust it and change it. You're very careful that everything is rendered perfectly. So though you were focused on the table, the thing, you were actually focused the whole time on your spouse. You're doing it for them. It is the same way with the unceasing prayer.

Everything you do is for God, though your attention, your activity, is focused on the duties of life. This way there is no separation between your life and your prayer; they are woven together like threads in a tapestry.

Our Dear Lord said one time, "When you pray, go to your private room, and when you have closed the door, pray to your Father who is in that secret place" (Matt. 6:6). You know where that private room is? In your heart, your mind, your soul. When he said, "Close the door," he wasn't just talking about those isolated moments in your life when you have quiet. What happens when you have kids and a job and you're fighting traffic? Where is that secret place?

Most people would say: in this rat race world there is no peace, there is no quiet retreat for me to say my prayers. But as you read this you are all alone with God in that secret place. You are thinking of things in your past, the present moment, the future, and you are trying to apply these ideas to them — you're really alone there. And that's how it is all day long. This is that secret place that Jesus says you must close the door to. Now, the door of our mind is open to whoever or whatever we wish to open it up to — and you let a lot of garbage in there! Then you say you can't pray. Just take the garbage out and you'll be able to pray quite easily.

It is very simple to pray without ceasing. It means living in the Present Moment. That's all it takes, and you can do that wherever you are. Sometimes that union with God and that unceasing prayer is a prayer of anguish, a prayer of tears, or a prayer of joy.

FOUR DEGREES OF PRAYER

The Lord showed me that there are four degrees of prayer that are applicable to your life. The first is the *Prayer of Strength.* It comes when you begin to realize that God is your Father and you've got this vacuum in your heart. You're full of sin, you're full of anxieties and frustrations, and you have nowhere to go. The thirst you have gives you a sense of repentance, which enables you to "open the door" to God's heart. Then once you repent, comes a prayer of the heart.

The *Prayer of the Heart* looks at God with a humble heart saying, "Lord I leave everything to Your will. I love You enough to accept all the nos and all the yesses. The Prayer of the Heart demonstrates a deep commitment that you are going to live a

116

Christian life no matter the temptations or obstacles.

The next prayer is the *Prayer of the Mind,* where you begin to examine yourself. This is where dryness comes in — that kind of empty feeling where you sense that God is far away and He's not listening. Did you ever feel that way? It's a good sign because it calls us to rise to a higher spiritual level. The Prayer of the Mind helps us dig into our own conscience and rid ourselves of all the junk.

And finally there is the *Prayer of the Soul,* when you feel a very deep presence of God, a deep sense of love. You begin to sense God's presence in your neighbor. It's the Father in you loving Jesus in your neighbor. That's the highest form of prayer, because it's unceasing.

A PRAYER OF FRUSTRATION

Your car breaks down and you are awaiting a tow truck and no one will stop to help you. At this tense and aggravating moment you have an opportunity of a lifetime. It will never come again. Others will come, but that one is gone.

Now, you may be mad as a hornet. Fine. Be mad as a hornet. Frustration is just as much a part of holiness as ecstasy. *Because prayer is where you are at the moment.* That's why it's unceasing. Prayer is to say to God in the Present Moment, "I know you have something good for me in this."

With the frustration, with the tension you must still pray. I carry Maalox with me all the time; I eat my Tums with every meal, because when I hold my temper and try to keep my patience, it gets me right here in the gut. Because I love Him, my stomach's griping me and my liver's turning upside down.

You see, you could pray more than you realize. You could say, "Jesus, I give this to you," this disappointment, this misery. It means that you are attuned to God's wisdom and God's Will in the Present Moment. The more you do this, the more you pray without ceasing, the closer you will draw to God, and the closer He will draw to you.

PRAYING IN DARKNESS

Sometimes I am so cold and in such darkness that I merely look to Heaven and plead for light. That's a prayer of faith. A lot of people think that faith is all joy. Well, I don't. Faith is sometimes scary. There are many moments in life where you are uncertain about which way to go. That kind of

118

faith is hard. There's a type of darkness in Faith, not the darkness that comes from sin, but the darkness that necessitates trust.

A PRAYER OF HOPE

Sometimes I feel like all is lost. We've all felt that. We've all felt like "it's finished," "we're bankrupt." Some of you are spiritually bankrupt. What do you do at those moments? I look up and say, "I put all my trust in You." That's a prayer of hope. Try it sometime.

CONTEMPLATIVE PRAYER

Contemplative prayer is to be absorbed in God.

The height of contemplative prayer is to have your heart with God . . . Just to stand before the Lord in loving presence with your mind totally blank is the highest form of prayer, and sometimes we squash that because of our pride. Our pride tells us we ought to be doing something. When we get to a high form of prayer, God does it all, and we are content to be humble in His presence.

WHO'S REALLY DEAF?

I feel sorry for those who cannot hear, who are physically deaf, but they hear more than we do sometimes. They hear the Lord in their silence. We are deaf to Him, though we hear.

Our Lord kept saying over and over, "He who has ears to hear, let him hear" (Luke 8:8). So obviously, it's not the organic structure of the ear that allows the sound to come in, it's the act of listening. And I don't think we listen to God or to His Scripture.

THE LANGUAGE OF SILENCE

The Spirit speaks many languages, but perhaps the most important is the language of silence. You want to try speaking to God that way sometimes. Quiet your mind, stop thinking about what you must say, and be still. Do nothing but realize for a few moments the essence of God. This language of contemplative silence can utterly annihilate you and sensitize you to the Presence of the Lord. When the soul and spirit prostrate themselves before God, realizing their own nothingness, many words are heard, but not spoken.

The Invisible Presence of God

Although you do not see God with your eyes, which is the lowest kind of vision, you can be aware of His presence in your heart and soul.

The invisible presence of God must be as real to you as the chair you are sitting on. That's what the Lord meant when He said, "As you have believed, so be it done to you" (Matt. 8:13).

My actions toward the visible — people, things, nature — must be guided by the vision I have of the invisible reality: the presence of the Lord in my soul.

A doctor practices medicine. You don't practice the Presence of God. You *become aware* of His presence. Faith reveals that He is in me. I have only to be still long enough to become aware of His presence and converse with Him. But His presence is not dependent on me.

The World's Peace and God's

The world's peace is always an absence of something or someone. You would have peace if your wife would go see her mother. You would have peace if you weren't working in this place, with these people. But the peace of Jesus is always a presence, a presence of Someone, not an absence.

NEW AGE SPIRITUALITY

The whole concentration of today's spirituality is upon the self. All of this transcendental meditation, all of this centering prayer is self-hypnosis. The whole thing is to do something for *you*. It has nothing to do with contemplation of God in your mind and heart.

MOTHER ANGELICA'S FAVORITE MEDITATION

There is dead time in your day that you could use to pray. People say, I don't have time to pray. Sure you do. Sometimes I think of an incident in the life of Jesus, and I imagine myself as part of that moment. We call it mental prayer.

My favorite mental prayer is Our Lord undergoing His agony in the Garden. It's a very beautiful way to meditate because every one of you reading this has endured some sort of mental anguish. Perhaps someone you loved has died, or you are going through a divorce and the children are torn between you and your spouse, or you are contending with a terrible illness. At those times of anguish and tragedy the agony in the Garden would be a good place to go.

Just close your eyes and visualize Our Lord walking in the garden where He has walked a hundred times. He kneels next to this huge rock. He leans on the rock for support and begins to cry. We all know what it is like to have loneliness, or tragedy, or poverty squeeze tears from our eyes — Jesus knew too. He also knew everyone who would be saved and all who would be lost throughout the ages. It squeezed blood out of His pores. That's a good meditation. You can see it in your mind's eye. Do it the next time you feel miserable and at the end of your rope. You will find consolation in that meditation. I promise.

NAME-DROPPERS

Today, when Christians want something, they become namedroppers: "Give this to me, in the name of Jesus," "Grant it to me right now, in the name of Jesus," they say. But it is not about that. We need to be so attuned to the Will of God that we only ask for the things that He desires, then we will get all we ask.

PRAYING IN HIS WILL

When you pray in faith, St. John tells us, you are in the presence of God by the act of prayer. He is listening to you as if there were no other creature in the whole wide world.

Faith tells me God has heard me the first time, and after he has heard me, I can release it to Him. If we ask Him for anything from a conversion to a printing press and *it is in accordance with His Will,* He will hear us. Certainly, the conversion is His Will. He wants His children to go to heaven, but you're going to have to let God do it. The printing press is another matter. But if He hears you, and it is His Will, He will accomplish it for you.

THE SECRET TO PRAYER

People didn't know how to pray, so Jesus came to teach us. What did we do? We would say, "O Creator of all things, I need such and such . . ." But Jesus said, "Our Father, who art in heaven . . ." (Matt 6:9–15). Prayer should be a very personal thing, a very loving thing.

In the Our Father there are only seven words there that say, "I want something": "Give us this day our daily bread." That's it. Everything else in the Our Father is praise and glory. You're asking for the Father's will to be done and for the grace to forgive. The secret to prayer is to spend most of the time praising God. You can ask for what you need, but afterward make sure you ask for God's Will to be done, and praise Him.

PRAYING FOR LITTLE THINGS

Every time you need cash, every time you need a favor from God, you go to that automated teller that you call "prayer," and you punch a few keys and you tell God what you want. Then you stand back and expect it. Prayer should be much more than requests. You must develop a rapport with God.

You know, if I get a new pair of shoes, I go into the chapel and show the Lord. I say, "Look at my shoes. Thanks a million." He gave me those shoes, after all. Now, you can do that in your daily life. You can pray for sunshine, or a quiet day, or a parking spot (they're near miraculous). Pray for little things, because little things say "I love you." Little things tell God that you trust Him.

MOTHER ANGELICA'S APPROACH TO PRAYER

I have a special relationship with Jesus. He's my Savior, my love, and I talk to Him, as a friend would speak to a friend. I speak to the Spirit as an intimate confidant, a friend you can talk to about anything. You have to remember, the Church teaches that when you speak to One member of the Trinity, you speak to the entire Trinity. There is no jealousy among them. So pick the Father, Son, or Holy Spirit, and start talking.

THE LEAST SIGNIFICANT PRAYER

One afternoon, Mother Angelica was trying to repair a piece of machinery in the monastery print shop. For an hour she repeatedly dropped an Allen screw into the gears. When she finally positioned the thing just so, Mother Angelica's phone rang. Startled, she lost the screw again, and decided to take the call.

So I went to the phone — not in a very good mood — and this woman told me her story. I went back to find my little screw, and a month later I get a check for $1,000 in the mail. So I called up the woman. I said, "I got this check in the mail today. Is this a mistake?" She said, "No. Don't you remember I called last month around two o'clock in the afternoon?" I'm thinking: The day of the Allen screw!

The woman said, "Remember I asked you to pray for my daughter's boyfriend. He was wrestling with another boy, hit his head on a rock, and was unconscious for days. The doctors thought he was going to be a vegetable. I called and asked for prayers, and a couple of hours later he woke up, ate a meal, and he's back in school." At that moment I remembered something. I remembered very distantly saying to the Lord, "Lord, would you get this kid out of dodo land?" What I'm trying to say here is never, never minimize the power of the least significant prayer, because God hears you. And some of you, He'd be so tickled to hear your voice at all.

HUNGER AND SPIRITUAL DRYNESS

If God wants to draw me higher spiritually, He has to create a situation in which I can get there. He creates a hunger within you, and you yearn for spiritual food. The only way to feed your soul, to mold it and change it, is to give you this hunger. You must absolutely have a hunger before God can grow in your soul. It is necessary for you to have dryness in prayer.

Don't judge your interior life or your prayer life by dryness. Dryness is a necessary pain. We need to love God for Himself, not for the feelings we experience because of Him. Our Dear Lord loved His Father more on the cross than at any time in His human life. Dryness is the sign of God's pleasure. It means that He wants to push you higher and higher to the realms of serenity. Without consolations, He wants you to be convinced that He is your all.

DRYNESS IN PRAYER

Spiritual dryness is a gift from God, because it removes the soul from the emotional level and puts prayer on the level of the will, where I am a child of God who does the things of God because I decide to do so, not because I am depending on emotions outside of me.

I've had spiritual dryness for thirty-three years. But I praise God for it, because I have learned something. When I go into that chapel feeling miserable and dry with no desire to pray, I say, "Jesus, I love you and I am here just to praise You, to console You, to be in Your Presence." If I'm there looking at Jesus, that is a greater gift to God than if I were present all joyful and bubbly. Everyone responds to consolation. *It's responding to God when you don't feel like it that will get you to heaven.* The terrible feelings should not make you experience guilt; in fact they purify and perfect your offering of love.

Recognizing the Trinity: An Exercise

We are going to do something with the understanding that God lives within you. You have in your soul three distinct persons loving each other. I want you to close your eyes and become aware of God loving Himself — you are out of the picture entirely; forget the self. You are loving God purely free of personal desires.

Now let that act of God loving Himself touch you. Eventually your heart will find itself in the eternal embrace of the Trinity. Five minutes of that kind of prayer will do more for your soul than anything else. Like a child you are observing the pure love of God and are a part of it. Remember what the Scripture says, "Whoever remains in Me, with Me in him, bears fruit in plenty" (John 15:5).

Detachment

Detachment from the things of the world is a necessary prerequisite for any spiritual growth. Mother Angelica explained it to her sisters this way:

Detachment is an overwhelming attachment to God.

Experiencing the Spirit of God

We do not see God because we are so busy looking at things or at ourselves. But we must seek the Spirit of the Lord, because without His Spirit there is no holiness, there is no happiness, there is no joy, there is no contentment, there is no realization of a mission in life. There is only emptiness and confusion. So when you look into your individual lives and ask what's wrong, perhaps you should begin by looking within and see how close you are to the Spirit. How aware are you of the Spirit working in your soul?

You Are a Temple

The first Christians were so caught up in this great gift the Master left us, the Advocate, the Holy Spirit, that it is all they could speak about. They would often say, "The Spirit has led me to do this." The Spirit of the Lord is beauty and holiness. The Spirit is an invisible reality that we experience.

How vast is God, and how marvelous that this God who is totally self-sufficient willed to create me to give Him glory. And to think that we are temples of the Lord, that He would want to be in such a small, soiled thing as my soul.

Today I notice a lot of people have lost hope. They've lost hope in the government, in their leaders, in their churches. We are getting to the place where the first Christians were, a state of despair. I think we have a magnificent opportunity of participating in the coming of the Spirit in the same way the first Christians did. In the last supper discourse (John 16) Our Dear Lord said, "The Advocate, the Holy Spirit, whom the Father will send in my name, will teach you everything." You see, the coming of the Spirit was the very reason Jesus Himself came. He came to redeem you — and redemption is not just going to Heaven, it means a complete change in your life, so that you become something you were not. It is the work of the Spirit to transform you into the image of the Father, the Son, and the Holy Spirit.

The Lord did not take the first Christians out of their surroundings, He left them where they were and gave them a power to rise above themselves. You have that same power.

Fear of the Lord

The first gift the apostles received (referenced in Isa. 11:2) was fear of the

Lord. Now, you might say, "I don't want to be afraid of the Lord." Well that is not what it means. There are two reasons to fear: out of punishment or out of love. If you love someone deeply, you do not want to hurt them in any way. You will do anything to avoid offending them. That's what fear of the Lord is: a childlike fear, rooted in love.

This fear of the Lord gave the apostles a deep knowledge of God as Father. They had the experience, through the power of the Spirit, of being sons of God, and they would do nothing to offend their Father. It drove them, and hopefully will drive us, to imitate the Father's mercy and compassion. When I am a child of God I must desire to be like the Father.

This spiritual gift informs us that God is truly our Father and enables us to look upon all mankind as brothers and sisters, children of the same Father. We have the same concern for our brothers and sisters as the Father has. Without making this leap, taking this spiritual step, there can be no other. This gift enables us to rise above our human nature. It teaches us to love like God loves.

The fear of the Lord even elevates temptation. Temptation ceases to be negative, but becomes positive. You no longer think: I can't do this because I'll go to hell or I'll get caught. No. You now refrain from doing wrong because you love our Father and our Father would be displeased. It's about love and it frees you.

This gift of the fear of the Lord is like an aid to keeping the first commandment to love God the Father with our whole heart and mind and soul and strength.

Piety

To love is to wish one well and to do all you can to bring that about. The gift of piety resembles the virtue of love. It gives me a childlike affection for God. I am obliged to love as God loves me. My love for you must be totally separated from whether or not you are lovable.

Through this gift you can see people in a totally different light. For instance, when you analyze why you don't like people, you will find it is because they do not do what you expect them to do, they do not give what you expect them to give, they do not please you. But if you love as God loves, you are not disappointed in anyone, because you know human nature.

The gift of piety makes me love. What is love? Love is an intangible desire, a giving of the self, something that makes me change for the better. "God is Love," St. John says (1 John 4:8). When I love Him as Father, a part of that love comes into me — it *is* the Spirit. And when the Spirit of the Lord enters into my heart, He transforms me; He makes a new creation; a new mind, a new heart. Love makes us new.

So my love for you must make you new, it must change both of us. You cannot possess God's love and give it to others without changing that person in some way. If your neighbor is not changed for the better because he knows you, you do not love him, you love yourself! The greatest witness of the first Christians was their love. "See how these Christians love each other," people said. We must love like that.

The gift of piety should do another thing for you. It should allow you to release everyone to the Lord. The gift of piety makes you look upon everyone as someone very precious with an immortal soul. It protects me from judging others. So every day ask the Spirit of the Lord to give you a great degree of the gift of piety that you might have patience and compassion, that you might love first and never be disappointed. Because, remember, as you love your neighbor, so you love God.

Fortitude

The third gift of the Holy Spirit, given to us at Baptism, is the gift of fortitude. It is very powerful. To have fortitude is to have courage. But courage for what? Fortitude to my mind is very akin to faith, because I must sincerely believe that Jesus is Lord before I have the guts to do what a Christian must, when everyone is doing something else. I must have the courage to stand alone, to be willing to be called a fanatic, and to leave my family and all my possessions for the sake of the kingdom. Not everybody is called to that. For some the greatest penance is staying where you are, but it takes a lot of courage to stay and still be what God wants you to be.

The fortitude that the Spirit grants us is much greater than a conviction. It is a drive. Our Lord had it in spades. When He was traveling one day with the apostles, He said, "I have a baptism by which I must be baptized and how I am *straitened* until it is accomplished" (Luke 12:50), meaning he could hardly wait for that moment when He would redeem us. That is fortitude.

A Christian is never really afraid of persecution; he is straitened until it occurs. You know our Lord said some very odd things. The Beatitudes are the wildest things in the whole wide world. He said, "Blessed are you when people abuse you and persecute you and speak all kinds of calumny against you on my account. Rejoice and be glad, for your reward will be great in heaven" (Matt. 5:11–12).

Now we come to the thing that keeps most of us from sharing in this gift of fortitude: human respect. I know what God wants me to do or say at this moment, but I am afraid of so and so. Now some say we have to be prudent. But one thing we have too much of today is prudence. We are all so careful; I don't think people have to worry about prudence. Do you notice how you are hemmed in by human respect? You're so afraid of what other people will say, or think, or feel that you deny God His will. With the gift of fortitude you couldn't care less. There is only one thing in your mind: to know Him, to love Him, and to serve Him at this moment.

Look at Peter in the courtyard. He was terribly concerned about what those people in the courtyard thought of him. He didn't want them to know he was a Galilean. He didn't want them to know that he was a follower of that Man. What a perfect example of human respect. In order to prove to these people that he did not "know the Man," he swore and cursed. He became what they were, so they would not think of him as one of the twelve. He descended to their level out of human respect. What a magnificent example of change. Peter had a very weak faith, but after Pentecost he is the one who goes out and preaches the word without fear. The cord that held him down all his life was broken thanks to this gift of fortitude. He no longer feared what anyone thought. The mission given to him by Jesus was everything.

The gift of fortitude makes us persevere in holiness. It gives us the strength to forge ahead in the face of opposition and weakness. It gives us supernatural endurance, a spiritual daring. St. Paul in Second Corinthians describes it this way: "We prove we are servants of God by great fortitude in times of suffering, in times of hardship and distress; when we are flogged, or sent to prison, or mobbed; laboring, sleepless, starving. We prove we are God's servants by our purity, knowledge, patience, and kindness; by a spirit of holiness, by a love free from affectation" (2 Cor. 6:4–6).

Fortitude is not only accepting the cross that God gives you, it is to empty yourself and to be unashamed that you love Jesus. This is a gift we must pray for every day, for when we lack fortitude we lack hope and faith and love.

We need to tell the Holy Spirit: Let me know the Father as He is, and let me love Him as a child. Let me love my neighbor in the same way You love me. Then let me be strong. No matter what anyone says, or thinks, or does, let me persevere. Let me be unashamed that I am a Christian. Amen.

Counsel

The next gift of the Holy Spirit is logical. Once I have the first three gifts I need discernment because there will be times in my life when I will not know God's Will. I have to discern. There is an enemy that is bent on your eternal destruction, and he uses people to trip you up, to lead you astray. There is a gift that God has given you, at Baptism, by which you can discern who and what is for your good. It is the gift of counsel.

The gift of counsel tells me what to judge and what not to judge. I am to judge by fruit, "by their fruits, you shall know them" (Matt. 7:20). To "know" is to experience, and when you have experienced the evil in someone else's life, when that evil touches your life and makes you doubt God's existence or providence, that is bad fruit. You have not judged the individual, you have *experienced* the evil in his life — the fruits. Places can be evil too. Inanimate places that breathe out darkness. Your spirit recoils when you go near them. No Christian can pass a massage parlor and not feel the evil that emanates from that place. This is not judging, it is discernment. Your spirit is discerning what is there. If the Lord died for you, do you believe He would leave you a sheep among wolves with no alarm system, with no discernment, no counsel to distinguish right from wrong?

When you are inspired to something by the Lord, the gift of counsel clears away the uncertainty. If God is guiding you to do something for Him and for His kingdom all hell will not stop you.

The gift of counsel also gives us self-knowledge. It gives us the light to see ourselves as we are. Some evening write on a piece of paper everything you have found fault with in someone else today, and you will see, on that paper, a description of yourself head-on. Unless something is in you, you can't see it in anyone else. You think everyone is a liar, because you are a liar. The husband thinks his wife is stepping out on him, because he's stepping out on her.

If you don't know yourself, how are you

going to prune yourself? If you don't prune yourself, God must permit those events in our lives that almost crush us. God in His Mercy and the Spirit with His magnificent gift of counsel permit things to happen in your life to reveal who you really are — to make you conscious of an interior fault, a weakness, an imperfection, a sin. Then you can do something about it before your time comes. Counsel is that gift of God by which we first know ourselves and then are able to discern the human spirit, the Holy Spirit, and the evil spirit operating in our lives.

Knowledge

Knowledge is that gift of the Holy Spirit that detaches us. We often think of knowledge as the acquisition of a particular discipline or subject. But the gift that the Spirit gives us is knowledge of how God thinks, how He regards life and things. It gives me an insight into the transitory nature of all that is created.

The gift of knowledge puts heart in your Christianity. Many good people live a Christianity of the mind where they profess Him with their lips. But Paul said that isn't enough; to be saved, Jesus must be accepted by my heart (Rom. 10:9). If your Christianity is only an acceptance of truth and an ethical code, then your Christianity is in the mind. The danger there is, when something befalls you, you cannot understand it. Your religion is in peril. Our minds cannot reason everything out; pain and suffering and famine, for instance . . . The gift of knowledge helps me find the pearl of great price buried in the soil of adversity. The gift of knowledge gives me awareness of the one thing necessary in this life: my union with God and His kingdom. It makes us realize that we do not have here a lasting city. This is not home. The early Christians knew this and we have forgotten it, or perhaps never knew it. Being healthy, wealthy, and wise was not their life's goal. The gift of knowledge helped them see that this life is a temporary testing ground.

This gift, that we must nurture and make grow in our hearts, leads to an utter detachment from everything. There are things we must accomplish in this life, and people we must love, but we cannot become attached to them all.

Our whole lives are hampered by things and people and ourselves, but with the gift of knowledge I am not hampered by anything. If I have friends, I give them to God. If I have things and they make me happy and suddenly they are gone, I give those to

God as well. We must be detached from everything.

I know a woman, and the first thing she did when she bought a new table was to take a piece of glass and scratch it. She knew she had this hang-up. She was so focused on having a perfect table that she couldn't concentrate on the people around her table. So she scratched it, gave thanks to God, and she had peace. That is utilizing the gift of knowledge. I have to have that disposition that I can live in the world and love it and see it and enjoy it, but never lose sight of heaven. I can have things and have them taken away with equal grace, because it's not permanent. The thing that is really valuable, the wealth that time cannot consume is waiting for me in the kingdom.

The gift of knowledge is detachment and hope. It is that balance of the spiritual with the human, between life here and the life to come.

Understanding

Let's look at the gift of understanding. How many times in your life can you say that your will was totally united with God's? Has there ever been a time when you could perfectly understand God's plan? If you have, then you have really made progress.

You've begun to think as God thinks and plan as God does. Every time you have read Scripture and gotten something new from it, every time you looked at something and saw the spiritual meaning behind it, every time you have been intuitive and suddenly realized an invisible reality, you have exercised the gift of understanding.

Scripture is the place where the gift of understanding is very important. Remember when Christ explained the Eucharist to the crowds. The Lord said, "He who eats my flesh and drinks my blood has life everlasting" (John 6:56–57). And Scripture reports that they walked away, they did not understand. Jesus looked at His apostles and said, "Do you also wish to go away?" Peter said, "Lord, to whom shall we go?" (John 6:68). Peter understood what the crowds did not. Why was that? Because the minds, the hearts of these apostles sought the Lord. If you are seeking the Lord, you already have understanding. If you know what you need, you already have understanding.

This gift gives you intuitive vision: knowledge that you have not acquired by any visible means, not by a book or someone telling you. It is intuitive, directly from God — like a beam from God to your soul. When things are hard in your life, the Spirit will

bring the word of Jesus to your mind —
that's the gift of understanding. The Spirit
of the Lord is so quiet, so elusive. He comes
in the midst of such turmoil and chaos, if
you are not listening you are liable to miss
it. That's why you need at least five minutes
of absolute silence, dead silence, so you can
open up the valve of your mind and the
door to your heart and say, "Lord, flood me
with Thy grace and Thy words." Then along
comes an idea of how to apply a particular
piece of Scripture to your unique situation.
That's understanding in operation. It means
I see how God is working in my soul. In
this beautiful gift of understanding, faith is
increased.

Understanding is the root of contemplative prayer. It is at the root of the ability to
see Jesus everywhere. So a Christian looks
at a tree and he sees the Father, Son, and
Holy Spirit. He sees the hand of God in
everything. He sees into the mystery of
God's ways and will. He understands as
God understands. St. Peter says, to attain a
participation in the divine nature, "you have
to do your utmost yourselves, adding goodness to the faith that you have" (2 Peter 1:5–
6). You need to understand God's ways to
be good.

This beautiful gift of understanding, the

gift that makes you pray and gives you an intuition into the very Spirit of God, will make you productive and help you bear much fruit for God.

Wisdom

The kind of wisdom that the Lord gives you is not discernment. The wisdom that God gives us is God Himself. St. John says, "In the beginning was the Word and the Word was with God and the Word was God . . . All things were made by Him and without Him was made nothing" (John 1:1,3). In the book of Wisdom, God is personified — the incarnate Word is personified by the word "Wisdom." So God is wisdom. You can't say He possesses wisdom or has wisdom. God *is* wisdom.

So when we speak of the gift of wisdom we are speaking of God giving us Himself. When we receive from the Holy Spirit the gift of wisdom, we receive in a very special way the Divine Indwelling. That's what the gift of wisdom is all about: Father, Son, and Holy Spirit living in me.

That's why the mystics and the saints had such a horror of sin. Because it is sin that snatches away the Spirit of the Lord and makes a man devoid of God, and that's a lonely way to be.

Wisdom gave the apostles at Pentecost something they never had before, and that was a deep awareness of the presence of the invisible God within them. They knew in the very depths of their souls that they possessed God. People could see it in their eyes, in the joy on their faces, in their courage and suffering. There was something so real, so above anything they had seen before. It was love. It was a tangible drive, an awareness, an experience of God.

You have been given the same gift. It provides you with a deep assurance that you are constantly in the arms of God. He is so close.

Wisdom is that gift by which and through which you somehow go into God and become one with Him. It's a mysterious gift, which ties together and encompasses all the other gifts of the Spirit. Wisdom reaches into counsel, that discerning self-knowledge, and raises me up to be a son of God. Wisdom reaches into fortitude and gives me strength of soul to suffer, to die, to live, to laugh, to cry with love. Wisdom sees knowledge as that total detachment from every created thing, ever reaching up and out to God. Wisdom reaches into Scripture and sees things there no one sees; it discerns God's hidden meaning in every verse.

Wisdom helps me see God as my God, Jesus as my Jesus, my Savior. It's very personal. St. Paul says He "lived and died for me." It gives me such a personal relationship with Jesus as Redeemer and Sanctifier, as if I were the only person in the world. There is between myself and God, thanks to this gift, a total aloneness, and it reaches into the very depths of the heart and the soul.

A Summary of the Gifts

Every day you use these gifts of the Holy Spirit, whether you know it or not. It's like breathing; you're not conscious of it, but you do it constantly — at least I hope you do. Peter says a strange thing in his second epistle. He says these gifts are a "guarantee of something . . . wonderful to come." He said, "You will be able to share the divine nature and to escape corruption in a world that is sunk in vice" (2 Peter 1:4).

These gifts are finally a participation in the divine nature of God — and the manifestation of that nature in your life will draw others and bear much fruit. Remember what Jesus said at the Last Supper, "He who abides in Me, and I in him . . . will bear much fruit" (John 15:5). And you will.

The Eighth Gift of the Holy Spirit

The sisters say I have the eighth gift of the Holy Spirit: guts!

Morning Ablution

We should try to incorporate little reminders of holiness into our day. For instance, I decided some time ago to wash my face with water seven times in the morning; to just splash water in my face, and on each splash I would ask the Holy Spirit for one of His seven gifts. So I ask Him for the fear of the Lord during the first splash. And on the second one I ask for piety, on the third I ask for fortitude, until I get them all. I knock it out until I get to faith, hope, and love.

Now, it is not holy water, and there is nothing magical about washing your face, but water and spirit seem to go together, and that little action reminds us of the gifts that can be ours. We need something definite that the mind and body can focus on to constantly remind ourselves to ask for these precious gifts.

The Consuming Spirit

The faith should be like fire to a piece of paper. The fire does not leave the paper untouched. It transforms it into ashes. The Holy Spirit is very much the same. It transforms and consumes us, or it should.

THE DIGNITY OF A CHRISTIAN

The Lord came so that you and I might be a temple of His Spirit. Can you imagine that God, Who created the universe and all its majesty, is inside of you? That truth is your witness and you must be aware of your full dignity. I wonder if we are not changing the world because we have lost sight of the crucial truth that God is within us?

CHARISMATIC

The word *charism* means a gift for others. If you apply the word *charismatic* to yourself, you're having a dream session. Because you can't decide you're charismatic; other people have to do that, for the simple reason that they either experience something good in you, or they don't. The real charismatic doesn't know they're charismatic. It only means that there is a gift here that somehow brings others closer to the Lord.

REFLECTING GOD

It isn't who you are or what you are or how good or bad you are, you have been commissioned by God to reflect one of His attributes. Some of you will reflect the mercy of God by forgiving. Some of you will reflect the silence of God. Some will reflect the sweetness of God. You are to bear fruit for the glory of the Father. By conforming yourselves to God's Will, you reflect, in a very small way, some of the beauty of God.

"With our unveiled faces reflecting like mirrors the brightness of the Lord, all grow brighter and brighter as we are turned into the image that we reflect. This is the work of the Lord who is Spirit" (2 Cor. 3:18).

THE PRAYER OF THE SPIRIT

St. Paul says we do not even know how we are praying; the Spirit helps us in our weakness and the Spirit prays in us, in words known only to God: inaudible words, unsaid words, yearnings in our souls.

UNAFRAID OF REALITY

This is the whole tenor of today's world: hug yourself, drink yourself into oblivion. All they do is constantly try to forget what is wrong, to obliterate what is wrong with us. But you see, when the apostles were filled with the Holy Spirit, they got something they didn't have before: joy and knowledge and all the gifts of the Holy Spirit. They had the same problems they had before: the Pharisees were still after them; they were still being persecuted. They didn't forget their problems; they went out to meet them. That is what a Christian is supposed to do. And that is one of our witnesses.

You are now a free people, a holy people. You are unafraid of pain or sorrow. You feel it, but you're not afraid of it.

GRACE AND NATURE

Grace builds on your human nature; it does not destroy it. The Spirit lives in me, and that Spirit enables me then to make right choices. Even though I fail, and I fail often, grace gives me the ability to rise and begin again.

HUMILITY: A PROTECTION AGAINST EVIL

Humility, spiritually speaking, is a protection. Look at the Son of God. Lucifer never saw Him coming because he could not imagine, in his pride, that the Son of God would be born in a smelly, stinking stable. I mean, that really fooled him. The smart aleck didn't catch on. Then when the Holy Family fled to Egypt to escape from Herod,

151

Lucifer had to think: "Aw, that can't be the Son of God. He wouldn't run from anybody." Lucifer never caught on because the Lord was so humble. Satan doesn't know humility and he doesn't know the truth.

EXAMINATION OF CONSCIENCE

Before you go to bed, examine your conscience a little bit and ask yourself if you were like Jesus today. Maybe you lost your temper, swore a little bit, looked at something you shouldn't have. Go back and apologize to anyone you offended, and then ask the Lord to forgive you. At the nearest opportunity go to Confession — the Lord will forgive you and guide you. We all need that grace, and it begins with an honest evaluation of where you are spiritually.

SPIRITUAL GENEROSITY

In the world, whenever you give something away, you lose it. But in the spiritual life, in the life of holiness, whatever you give comes back to you again and again, and it grows and multiplies. Think of a star in the sky. I see it and point it out to you. When you look at it, I have not lost it. I still have the star, and the joy of it, and something more: I have the joy of you beside me.

7
THE POWER AND MEANING OF PAIN AND SUFFERING

So many "teachers of the Gospel" approach pain and suffering theoretically, if at all. Yet they remain the most constant of human experiences. Though few of us have ever known spiritual ecstasy or received a vision of a saint, during say, breakfast, none of us is untouched by suffering.

Suffering has been integral to the path of Mother Angelica. It is central to her charism, the source of her greatest accomplishments, the cornerstone of her life and thought. She has struggled with diabetes, a bloated heart, a twisted spine, lame legs, and asthma, among other maladies. She did not merely expound the teachings that follow, she lived them.

Over time, Mother developed a rather so-phisticated philosophy of pain and suffering. These ideas, thoughts, and prayers helped her sanctify the pain in her own life, and prof-fered hope to those coping with physical, mental, or spiritual hardships of their own. Here are a few of her insights for those difficult moments of suffering that inevitably come to us all.

PAIN AND SANCTIFICATION

Pain is part of our sanctification. How are you going to be like the Lord if you don't have the opportunity to shed those things that are controlling you, diverting you from holiness? Pain is that opportunity.

THE PREPARATION OF PAIN

As I look back, pain was always a preparation for me. The Lord allowed pain before accomplishing anything He asked me to do. It made me more aware of my own weaknesses, my own faults, my own incompetence, my own lack of knowledge . . . it made me appreciate the fact that God must do everything.

THE PERFECT IMAGE IN PAIN

The Church has taught and shall continue to teach that pain and suffering are either ordained or permitted by God. In those who suffer, the Father sees the perfect image of His Son.

Suffering in itself is neither good nor bad.

It is the *way* one suffers and the *fruit* of that suffering that matters.

TRUSTING GOD WITH PAIN

As children of a loving Father, we must trust His wisdom regarding the kind of cross that is necessary for the purification of our particular weakness. Only He knows the degree of glory He desires for us and what graces and sufferings are needed to arrive at that sublime destiny.

THE PURPOSE OF SUFFERING

Mother Angelica believes suffering has a purpose in our lives. During her private lessons she would often direct her charges to this Scripture quote for the answer:

"The purpose of it is that you may be found worthy of the Kingdom of God; it is for the sake of this that you are suffering now" (2 Thess. 1:5).

OBEDIENCE

Love is proved by obedience. And we must be obedient to pain and suffering as we are to joy and good times.

WASTED PAIN

Suffering in itself does not make us holy. It is only when we unite it, out of love, to the suffering of Christ that it has meaning. Suffering without love is wasted pain.

IT IS NOT FOREVER

No matter what suffering you have: physical, mental, spiritual — it will all pass, as everything passes.

THE POSSIBILITIES OF SUFFERING

When you are suffering you have the capability of achieving great things. You can:

1. Create great holiness and become a powerful witness to those around you.
2. By accepting your pain you are doing God's Will in an awesome way.
3. By offering your pain to God, you can save souls.

God is trusting you with pain; He is trusting you to accept it with love. Don't miss the possibilities.

THE TYPES OF SUFFERING

Preventive Suffering

God can use suffering to prevent us from committing sin, from making errors in judgment, from becoming worldly or proud. He at times will bless us with disappointment and frustration to direct us toward His path. This suffering prevents us from making the wrong choices and keeps us away from danger and evil, though we are often unaware of it as it is happening.

Corrective Suffering

When a person violates the law of God, the Commandments for instance, untold suffering follows. We cannot blame this suffering on God. It is the inevitable result of disobedience. Still, God loves us, and His love brings good out of every mistake we make. The suffering incurred by disobedience can be used to purify the very weakness that produced it. He uses the suffering to correct us and to return us to His ways.

Repentant Suffering

The suffering heart, broken over its infidelities, broken out of love for so great and good a God, is a sacrifice that rises to heaven and is accepted by God more than many good works.

Repentant suffering cleanses our souls, brings down upon us the compassion of God, and enables us to begin anew.

MOTHER'S PAIN AND OURS

I don't remember a day, even before I knew Jesus, when I didn't have a problem, when I didn't have a pain. And I realized that it was a privilege.

I know it's hard for you to understand what I'm saying, because the world tells you something else. But everybody suffers in the world. Whether I am suffering in a physical, mental, or spiritual manner, I resemble Jesus at those moments, and the Father looks at us in our pain and He sees His Son in the most beautiful way. That's what makes you holy. Don't rebel. We don't understand, but He didn't ask us to understand. He didn't say, "Blessed are those who understand." He said, "Take up your cross and follow me" (Mark 8:34).

It takes a lot of guts to endure pain all day long. Some of you have pain in your limbs, in your body, in your heart, in your mind — and there's no way that you can get away from it. But you can suffer with Jesus. This is why we have Our Lord on the cross. Not because we haven't taken Him down, but because you need a reminder that in your pain and suffering you've got Somebody with you. You've got Somebody in you. You've got Somebody holding your hand. You're not alone.

A Prayer During Pain

During most of her pain-filled life, Mother Angelica repeated a brief prayer that she would utter throughout the day. She told me it was one of her favorites.

> Lord, I offer this pain to You to save souls.

Sanctifying Pain

Yesterday I was trying to think of how to unite an infection I had with Jesus. I thought, "Boy this'll be a good one." And suddenly the thought came to me: When Jesus was stretched out on the cross, His legs pulled down, His arms stretched out, He must have had unbelievable pain in every organ. Unbearable pain. Suddenly the ordinary pain of my infection, something so common, became holy, it became sanctified.

A Beautiful, Painful Vision

I thank God for my pain. It brought me closer to Him and made me realize there's more to life than what I have and what I see.

Do you realize, my friends, the joy of Helen Keller? The very first voice Helen Keller ever heard was the voice of God. What a rarely considered blessing she had. She never heard an angry voice. She never heard insults. She couldn't hear.

Consider her blind eyes. She never saw a flower or a tree or the face of a child. The first face she saw was the face of God. Can you imagine the joy of Helen Keller? Is there anyone who can say that Helen Keller was deprived? For a brief time, yes. But for eternity, no. Her joy in heaven is everlasting.

You and I must learn to look beyond the suffering of these fleeting moments and *know* that we will soon have such joy and understanding. Our joy in heaven has God as its source, and it is forever.

The Healing Novena

When twenty-one-year-old Rita Rizzo (Mother Angelica) was suffering from stomach difficulties in 1943, her mother took her to visit a local mystic, in Canton, Ohio, a woman named Rhoda Wise. It was believed that Mrs. Wise possessed intercessory healing powers. In fact, she herself insisted that she had been the recipient of a miraculous healing at the hands of St. Therese and Jesus Himself. So intense was her prayer, on Fridays during Lent, the woman would begin to bleed from her head, hands, and feet. In time, hundreds would come to visit Rhoda Wise. They would claim miraculous healings due to her intercession.

Wise rarely touched the afflicted, but merely gave them a prayer card: a novena to St. Therese urging a divine healing. Rita Rizzo was given such a card on January 8, 1943. Nine days later her stomach troubles dissolved. Following is the prayer Rita and her family prayed for healing.

Novena Prayer to the Little Flower

O beautiful Rose of Carmel, St. Therese of the Infant Jesus, deign according to your promise to descend from heaven to visit those who implore you. Pour down on us in profusion those celestial graces that are symbolized by the shower of roses that Jesus your Spouse has put at your disposition. Your power is great with His heart. He can only listen and hear your prayer. I have then recourse to you, O St. Therese of the Infant Jesus, assist me in this circumstance. Speak for me to Jesus and to Mary and obtain for me to live a holy life and die a happy death. Amen.

St. Therese hear my prayer. Show your power with God and cure me if it be for the honor of God, and the good of my soul. Amen.

HEALERS

This comes from the late 1970s. During this address Mother revealed her personal approach to pain and the mystery of its presence in her life. She would be famously "healed" one more time in 1997 (see *Mother*

Angelica: The Remarkable Story of a Nun, Her Nerve, and a Network of Miracles, p. 270).

Three times in my life I have been physically healed of three very serious ailments, and yet God keeps me in pain and in a brace. I realized one day that those who continue to suffer may not be healed, because they are healers themselves.

The greatest gift God has given me since my vocation is pain; because I am a proud individual, and with the apostolate God has given us, and the work we must do, I need to be totally reliant on Him. And if I can stand before a crowd for hours and beg God to give me strength for one more moment, if I can smile through that and make them laugh, then I have spiritually healed, precisely because I have not been physically healed.

Suffering is healing. There are those who think the path to holiness is to be healed of your bodily suffering, but oftentimes God uses the suffering to change us and to heal our souls.

THE SUFFERINGS OF JESUS

All the misery of the world, past, present, and future, could never compare with the sufferings of Jesus. Whatever you are going through, He's been there first, and He did it out of love.

THE HEALING POWER OF SUFFERING

We're ashamed to suffer and we're ashamed of the cross. We're ashamed of Jesus dying on the cross. Most of us want health and wealth and wisdom and everything to be fabulous. Come off it! It isn't going to be. If you want to witness real faith, go see the guy with pain. If there's anybody who wants to be free of it, it's the guy suffering from it.

We've got to get a balance, a balance in our mind between the healing power of suffering and the molding power of pain and suffering. Pain can be redemptive. We must learn to accept suffering with resignation, with love, with deep faith. God sometimes loves you enough to stop you dead. He cares more for you than for your pleasure here. Don't fight the suffering that Jesus gives you. Pray to endure it, pray to be healed, pray that it may be taken away; but always with a deep humility of heart that appreciates that God loves you enough to prune you. He trusts you with pain and suffering. Can you imagine that?

CHRIST'S CROSS

Did Jesus go on a mountaintop and yell, "I love you, I love you"? No, He got on a cross, stretched out His hands, was nailed to that cross, and said, "I thirst" (John 19:28). For what? Water? No. He thirsted for your love.

Every cross we have brings us closer to the Lord because it detaches us. It's easy to have faith when times are good. It's in the cross that our faith is proven. Sometimes, when it just seems too heavy and you can't seem to carry it any longer, go to a church, before the Blessed Sacrament if you can, or just in your living room, and tell the Lord: "I thirst for Your love, for Your understanding. Give me strength. Give me courage."

WHY JESUS SUFFERED

Why would God want to be like us? Why did He come in human form? You know you are not compassionate unless you have in some way suffered. Jesus came down and suffered so He could be compassionate. St. Paul says, because Jesus Himself has been through temptation, He is able to help others who are tempted (Heb. 2:18). The purpose of suffering and evil and temptation in your life is to change you, to give you merit, to enable you to help others.

When you negate all suffering in your life, you are throwing out awesome opportunities to change.

MARY'S SUFFERING

Look at Our Lady, that magnificent woman. Is there anyone you ever heard of who suffered as much as she has? Having to run from a tyrant, having your Child born in a stable, finally presenting that Child in the temple and having Simeon say, "This Child is destined for the fall and the rise of many" (Luke 2:34). Whew, what mother would love to hear that? Losing Him for three days, finding Him for so many years, and then seeing Him humiliated by those who should have known Him and accepted Him and loved Him — seeing Him ostracized by His own. Finally, seeing His apostles run in fear, betray Him, and deny Him, and then to watch Him die on a cross. What woman suffered as much as she did? Who dares call pain evil?

Our Sweet Mother went through the darkness in the valley of the shadow of death over and over as an example for you and me. That's the kind of faith the Lord expects of us, that kind of total abandonment.

Our Lady suffered with her Son. You've got to suffer with her Son too, and so do I.

166

Jesus says, "Take your cross upon yourself, and I will help you with it. Learn of Me." We don't often think of God trusting us. When we have crosses and more crosses on top of them, He is trusting us. If you accept them obediently and go forward with His help, your soul is being purified bit by bit and becomes beautiful before the Lord.

REDEMPTIVE SUFFERING

I'm a believer in what the Church calls "redemptive suffering." St. Paul says, "This is a wicked generation and your lives should redeem it" (Eph. 5:16). He wasn't saying that Jesus' life and suffering needed our redemption, but he was saying that we need to cooperate with Jesus — to unite our suffering with His.

I've been sick all my life. I don't remember a day I wasn't sick with something. And I think that Our Dear Lord's hand was on me. I've had cross after cross from the earliest time I can remember. But it kept me dependent on the Lord to do whatever He asked me to do. The pain was a safety for me because I could never give myself credit for any accomplishment. It's a protection; it's like a shield for me. I think that's true of everybody; they just don't see it or they're not told about it. There's an obvious grace to being treated by the Father as He treated His Son for our sanctification and for the sanctification of other souls. We're so interested today in helping people and social work, why don't we help them to offer their pain and suffering up to God?

When we can't alleviate their pain, we need to give them a spiritual answer that strengthens them and teaches them that their pain and suffering is not only important, but also necessary to the world.

SUFFERING FOR ALL OF MANKIND

St. Paul tells us: "I am suffering now, and in my body, to do what I can to make up all that has still to be undergone by Christ for the sake of His body, the Church" (Col. 1:24). It's my body, but His pain. I don't know how many Christians realize that this is one of the greatest revelations that God gave us. It is Jesus who continues to suffer in the Christian for the good of all mankind.

Every pain we endure with love, every cross borne with resignation, benefits every man, woman, and child in the Mystical Body of Christ.

Pain and Redemption

Christ suffered to give you an example, not to take it away. We don't understand the power of Redemption. Before Redemption, man prayed to get rid of pain, and after, he prayed to endure it with joy. How much greater that is. Before Redemption, we needed God to answer all our prayers to prove He blessed us, but after Redemption, we look upon the Cross and know that when He puts it up on this shoulder, He has looked upon us as sons!

Eternal Words on Suffering

Though Mother rarely elaborated on this first Scripture verse, it appears to be one of her favorites. Again and again she returns to it like a safe harbor in her early talks and lessons. Even unadorned, the verse has a particular power, especially when one considers the near constant pain Angelica has borne throughout her life. It will no doubt be as encouraging to anyone suffering from chronic pain as it has been for the suffering abbess. Some of her other favorite Scripture quotes on this topic follow.

St. Peter says: "Think of what Christ suffered in this life, and then arm yourselves with the same resolution that he had: anyone who in this life has bodily suffering has broken with sin, because for the rest of his life on earth he is not ruled by human passions but only by the will of God" (1 Peter 4:1–2).

Put that in your coffee and stir it up a little bit.

St. Peter also said: "My dear people, you must not think it unaccountable that you should be tested by fire. There is nothing extraordinary in what has happened to you. If you can have some share in the sufferings of Christ, be glad, because you will enjoy a much greater gladness when His glory is revealed" (1 Peter 4:12–13).

"My brothers, you will always have your trials, but when they come, try to treat them as a happy privilege; you understand that your faith is only put to the test to make you patient, but patience too is to have its practical results so that you will become fully developed, complete, with nothing missing" (James 1:2–4).

St. Paul says that "As it was his purpose to bring a great many of his sons into glory, it was appropriate that God, for whom everything exists and through whom everything exists, should make perfect, through suffering, the leader who would take them to their salvation" (Heb. 2:10). Now, if Jesus was made perfect through suffering, are you under the impression that you, sinner that you are, will be made perfect any other way?

To Heaven with Defects

Next to my vocation, the greatest gift I have is the pain I carry every day because it forces me to cling to Jesus. When we ask for healing we should ask for healing in the way we need healing. Many ask for physical healing, but I think spiritual healing is more important. I can go to heaven with crippled legs. I can't get there being hateful or unforgiving.

The Grace to Endure the Cross

Let us ask Our Dear Lord for the graces we don't even know we need, the grace to endure the cross with serenity. I think that has to be one of the greatest gifts, and I'm sure nobody asks for it. We are all going to have crosses, so we need the grace to see God's hand in them — the grace to understand the economy of God.

Power in Weakness

God is looking for you. He is. His power is not great in somebody else's strength. His power is great in weakness, your weakness. So we all measure up.

> **Prayer When in Pain**
>
> Lord, I attach my pain to all of Your pain. I do not understand the mystery of pain, nor do I grasp the power of it to change a stubborn will like mine. Though I do not understand Your plan, my Lord, I accept it. I trust Your love and give You mine in the hope of being lost in Your embrace. Amen.

8
Overcoming Faults

There are imperfections and failings that dog all of us. Some can bar our progress and hold us back in the spiritual life. While offering spiritual guidance to her sisters, friends, and viewing "family," Mother Angelica often homed in on these peccadilloes and provided instructions for removing them from our lives. Her advice was ever perceptive and always direct. Perhaps her words will help you root out some of your own nagging little faults. Happy hunting.

To Give Glory to God

Overcoming our faults and weaknesses gives glory to God, because we can't possibly overcome them on our own.

A Lot of Leeway

In the Old Testament it says that the just man falls seven times a day, and in the New

Testament it's seventy times seven. It must be so hard to be a Christian that the Lord gives you a lot of leeway.

PUTTY IN HIS HANDS

Let yourself be putty in God's hands. You know, the same sun will harden one substance and melt another; it is because of the substance, not the sun. We are no different. Some harden their hearts when they get near the Son of God; other hearts soften. The love and grace of God pouring upon you day after day, moment by moment, is meant to mold you, not destroy you. Give in, and let God have His way with you. It's not a burden, it's a joy.

ADMITTING FAULTS

The only way to get to the Father's heart is to admit who you are, to know your weaknesses and your faults. This is where we fall short. Jesus died that you might live forever. Do you know anyone you would be willing to die for? Do you know anyone at all you would be willing to give your blood for? That's a lot of love. All He's asking in return is repentance for your sins and acknowledgment of your faults. That's a pretty good deal.

PERFECTIONISM

For souls plagued by perfectionism, who fret and anguish over tiny details, Mother offered a sage bit of advice. I can't tell you how often she directed this line to yours truly:

Don't let the perfect be the enemy of the good.

CRITICISM

Too often we criticize the person instead of their actions. We look at the sin and the sinner as one. That's where we make our big mistake with criticism. When we criticize — and I'm at fault too — the sin and the sinner become one in our mind. That is the difference between us and the Lord. He separates the sin out, but He still loves the sinner, passionately.

COMPLAINING VS. SHARING

I used to say to my mother, Sister David, "What are you complaining about?"

"I'm not complaining," she'd say. "I'm just talking."

"Well, your talking sounds like complaining," I'd say.

"Can't I share it with anyone?"

"Yeah, you can share it," I told her, "but

not twenty-five times in five minutes."

See, that's complaining. If someone has a headache and they tell you about it, fine. But then, if three minutes later it's: "Boy, this thing just won't go away." And seven minutes later: "I must have migraines or something." After you've said it once, it becomes a complaint. That's a good rule of thumb. Make your announcement and then keep the follow-ups to yourself. Nobody wants to hear that.

THE ENSLAVEMENT OF JUDGMENT

The Scriptures say "Judge not, and you shall not be judged" (Matt. 7:1). But then it says: "By their fruits you shall know them" (Matt. 7:16), which is to judge, isn't it? Well which is it, Lord? It means I cannot judge motives, intelligence, grace, and salvation. I can judge a fruit, and whether that fruit is going to affect me in the right way, but I cannot judge why someone does something. This is why we must love all men at the very least. Jesus is trying to liberate us from the enslavement of judgment.

JUDGE AS THE FATHER JUDGES

The Father judges no one until He calls them home. Did you ever think of that? He doesn't judge you at all in this life, so why should we?

GOSSIP

A woman told me she was giving up candy for Lent. I said, "I know something better. Why don't you fast from gossip?" She said, "What will I talk about?" So she tried it for a week, and she came back to me.

"I'm so nervous," she said. "I didn't realize it, but without gossip I have been absolutely silent. I don't have a thing to say." We do this because we convince ourselves that we are only "saying what's true." Well, you don't have to spread that kind of truth around. There is nothing lasting there. With gossip everything is a seven-day wonder.

EVEN TEMPERED

I'm Italian by nationality. We're very even-tempered — always mad! Sometimes I wake up in the morning impatient and angry. I would like to get up with vim and vigor, but I don't. Little things bother me. I get out of bed and I can't find my brace, or I can't find my shoes. Then one of my sweet sisters comes in and she says, "Good morning," with a big smile, a loving expression; and something happens to me. My bad temperament just melts away. See, love has power; it's a force with the power to heal.

STRESS AND TENSION

If you're experiencing stress or tension give it to Jesus. Tell Him, "I feel like crawling the wall, but I love You and I want to give this to You." Do you think our Lord wasn't tense living with those twelve screwball apostles?

BATTLING JEALOUSY

Jealous people are threatened by the talent, the position, even the intelligence of others. Their gifts actually cause the jealous person sadness. That's what happened to King Saul and David. Here comes young David, just a boy really, who slew Goliath and the people were rejoicing. They ran through the streets shouting, "Saul killed his thousand, and David his tens of thousands." What happened to Saul? He said, "All that David lacks is a kingdom and a crown." The Scripture tells us a cloak of darkness fell over Saul, and as he went along, the Spirit of the Lord left him (1 Sam. 18:6–30). You see, greed and selfishness and jealousy go hand in hand. You don't mind if somebody has something, so long as they don't have as much as you.

That jealousy will consume you, my friends, because it blots out light.

Do you know how to overcome that? The best way to overcome jealousy is to compliment your neighbor. Praise him. You'll soon begin to realize that everything your neighbor has and everything you have comes from God. Say a little prayer: "Lord, deliver me from jealousy. Make me bless my neighbor. Make me understand how unique he is and how unique I am. And let me be content with Your will in my life."

No One Is Perfect

When I was a young novice I used to pray in the early morning, "Dear Lord, today I am going to be patient come hell or high water." And by nine o'clock came hell and high water! I blew it!

Anger

When you are angry, love is leaving you. Anger, impatience, and criticism are the effects of the draining of love.

Anger Management

St. Jerome had a terrible temper. He would hit himself with a rock every time he lost his temper. I'd be dead as a doornail, with

179

no ribs, if I did that.

Confronting Our Faults

None of us are perfect, as hard as we try. Our faults and weaknesses are going to die fifteen minutes after we do. But this is something that we can give to Jesus. Every day I can make a choice to be like Jesus instead of like myself. Every day we have a chance to transform our soul. Keep trying. Holiness and virtue are a slow process. I've been a nun for more than half a century — how many things I wish I had done, and hadn't done . . . but the Lord knows I'm sorry. Tell Him, "Lord, I want to be like Jesus. I want to be holy. I want to see God. Help me be close to You, because with You I can reach that height." We have to be gentle with ourselves.

Sunset Anger

Did you ever notice how St. Paul said, "Do not let the sun set on your anger" (Eph. 4:26–27)? In the summer the sun sets later — so you've got extra time. God knows that some days it takes longer to get over it.

Prayer for Patience and Mildness

I went to Confession one time and I told the priest, "I lost my temper." He said, "Keep it, nobody wants it." Well, I never said "lost" again because I was afraid I'd get another smart-aleck comment.

I occasionally pray a little prayer that I wrote some time ago to help me out: "Lord, give me patience. It was a beautiful part of Your life. I need patience to use every spare moment to speak to You, to love You, and to meditate on Your attributes. Let me see the time I waste. Let me see waiting as the extra time allotted to me by Your infinite wisdom, to make me holy. Lord Jesus, hold my temper in your hands so I may not give it to others."

Patience

Patience is adjusting your time to God's time.

The One Thing Necessary

We all in a way harden our hearts a little bit; some to the point where they no longer hear the Word of God at all. There is always that one person that you haven't totally forgiven or loved with a pure love. There is still that one thing you won't give up for

Jesus. You are still capping your love. You do everything but this one thing. Well, do it today.

HATRED IN A COMMODE

So many of you have hatred for people, for years, over some silly thing. A woman came to me one time and she asked me to pray for her two daughters because they hadn't spoken to each other for two years. How do you like that? I figured something terrible must have happened. Turns out the woman's wealthy mother had died and she gave half of her fortune to one girl, and half to the other.

"What's wrong with that?" I said. "Why aren't they speaking?"

"They're arguing over a commode," the woman tells me.

"You mean a commode commode?"

"You don't understand," the woman says. "This is an inlaid commode."

"Oh wow! That must be some toilet," I say.

"It is," she says. "And they both believe they should have the commode."

"You go and tell your daughters that Mother Angelica said they should take turns putting their heads in it," I said.

Can you imagine going to hell and somebody comes up to you and says, "What are you in for?" And you say, "I got in over a commode." To harbor hatred and imperil your soul over something so trivial is sheer asininity; yet we do it every day.

PRIDE

Pride either keeps you back from doing what you should do for God and His kingdom or it pushes you forward into things you are not able to do.

UNDER THE INFLUENCE OF PRIDE

We often take pride in our work or in ourselves, meaning that we bathe and keep ourselves clean. That's a good kind of pride. The pride that is dangerous, the kind we are often unaware of, is deep in the soul, deep in the intellect, where egoism rears its head and the self takes its position on the throne. Family, friends, everyone becomes a servant. When under the influence of this pride we tend to find excuses for our bad behavior.

Our pride refuses to admit that we could be in any way guilty of what we are accused of. Rather than face the truth — which means we failed — we live a life of pretense. We begin to think that others are always at fault, and that we are perfect. Soon we can find ourselves living in a very false world.

WHAT PRIDE BREEDS

Pride is at the bottom of all worldliness: that desire that drives people to attain more and more things, more and more honor, more and more glory, of having the whole world revolve around themselves. Disobedience, rudeness, the lack of compassion toward our neighbor, all of this is pride. Selfishness is an effect of pride.

BANISHING PRIDE

In our walk with God, it is important that we never lose sight of our mission: to allow God to move in us without interference on our part. And that takes a lot of dying to self. When we kneel before a wafer of bread transubstantiated into the Body, Blood, Soul, and Divinity of Jesus, how can we justify our pride? Once you meditate on the humility of Jesus in the Eucharist, how can you possibly justify *your* pride?

Prayer to Heal Pride

O God, forgive us our pride; the pride that keeps us from radiating You. Heal my pride. Jesus, meek and humble, make my heart like unto Thine.

DOUBT

Doubt comes from pride. The proud believe they are supreme, and they have decided that things should be such and such in their lives. And when they are not such and such, there is no God. They put themselves on a mountaintop and look down on everyone. When the world does not satisfy their egos, they lose faith, and doubt sets in.

A SOLUTION FOR DOUBT

When I begin to doubt, and I wonder "How do I know it's all true?," I immediately turn to God and cry out, "I believe, O Lord, help my unbelief." The Lord never said we had to understand His will, or His truths. We only have to obey them. Don't worry if you have doubts. Doubts do not displease God. They are permitted by Him — permitted to bring out the depth of faith within us.

The Man Without Fear

I can't tell you how often I've been scared to death — how often I've said to myself: "Lord, am I being presumptuous or am I following You? Am I watching things evolve or am I thinking of all this myself?" But you see, don't worry when doubt hits your mind. That doesn't make you unworthy. That doesn't make you faithless. The man who has courage is not the man without fear, but the man who is out there on the front line, scared to death.

Stepping Past Fear

There was a brief moment when I hesitated during the taxing construction of Mother Angelica's biography. The research period was in its third year, and I could not see the end in sight. At that point, I considered the possibility of writing a small memoir and scrapping the goal of a full-scale biography. When I brought this idea to Mother's attention, her response was instantaneous:

If you want to do something for the Lord, do it! Whatever you feel needs to be done, even though you're shaking in your boots and you're scared to death — take the first step. The grace comes with that first step, and you get the grace as you step. Being afraid is not a problem. It's doing nothing when you're afraid, that's the problem.

Prayer for Us, the Fallen

Lord Jesus, as You fell the first time, we ask You to have mercy on all those who have moral weaknesses. After they fall over and over again, Lord, give them Your strength and courage. Give them grace to overcome their faults. Immaculate Heart of Mary, we entrust all sinners to Your care. Be their aid and comforter. Amen.

9
DEALING WITH TRIALS

It could be said that Mother Angelica has a PhD in trial management. From the time she was a young girl, she was inundated by familial and financial trials. Later, as a nun, physical trials consumed her. Then, at an age when most are playing shuffleboard and draining their IRAs, Mother Angelica stepped into the competitive world of cable television.

The trials never really stopped for Mother. Money was always scarce, her health always fragile, and someone was always gunning for her, yet she persevered. Her spiritual perspective on the trials of life saved her. The best of those insights follow. May they fortify you in your trials.

TRUE TROUBLE

The best sign in the world that God is ever-present in your heart and mind, that He is ever thinking of you, is when you have a problem. When you don't have any problems, that's when you should begin to worry.

The worst thing in the world is for God to leave you to your own devices with no opposition. When He lets you make mistakes, unimpeded, He has left you alone. And when God leaves you alone, you are truly in trouble.

TRIBULATION

I talked to a woman one time who had a lot of problems and finally I told her, "Give it to God." She put her hands on her hips and told me, "When the Lord gives you tribulation, He expects you to tribulate!" She was right. She couldn't read or write, but she knew more about the Lord than I did.

Don't feel bad or unworthy or unholy because you have frustrations, trials, heartaches, and pains. These are the things that God has allowed to perfect you. He is trying you, testing you, and often it takes time to overcome.

THE REDEMPTIVE POWER OF TRIALS

Know that when trials come your way they are meant to prune you. Don't say, "God is punishing me." God has more to do with His day than run around with a baseball bat hitting you over the head. You punish yourself. If you go around and drink two quarts of vodka, you can't blame God for the headache. You brought on the headache, which could be redemptive for you.

You have to first accept where you are with determination — determination that you are going to do more than change. You must begin to live a deeply spiritual life with Jesus, so that you can be transformed.

GOD'S BLESSINGS

We have a tendency to think that if we love God, and He loves us, He's going to bless us with the "good things of life." And He does. The problem lies in our definition of the "good things of life." Trials are sometimes as much of a good thing as a new car or health.

BECOMING A DIAMOND

You know, a diamond at one time was a piece of coal. By unbelievable pressure this ugly piece of coal is turned into a diamond. It's sort of like our interior lives. A lot of us are inundated by pressures, all permitted by the Lord, intended to transform us into spiritual diamonds. He wants to make all of us new.

Joyful Witness

When Our Lady appeared to St. Bernadette in Lourdes, she said to her, "I cannot promise you happiness in this life, only in the next." And believe me, poor Bernadette had a lot of joy but not very much happiness. Joy is an art really, a sharing of Faith.

See, if I possess something, I must share it. Faith allows me to maintain a spirit of joy in the midst of trials, and to show the power of God to those who don't believe.

Perfecting Us in His Way

We have preconceived ideas about how God is going to perfect us, and when he doesn't do it our way, we miss the boat. For instance, you asked for humility, you asked for gentleness, you asked for kindness, and He gives you opportunities to discover those virtues, and you fight tooth and nail.

How are you going to grow in faith if you don't have darkness? How are you going to grow in trust if there is no crisis? If you had a million dollars in front of you, would that make you trust? We're such a funny people. We have a possession concept: we're a people who acquire things, but the things of the Spirit must be earned through struggle.

LOVING YOUR ENEMIES

When she was a young sister in Canton, Ohio, Mother Angelica deeply disliked a certain sister in the monastery. She could not tolerate being near the nun, and avoided her like the plague. Sister Angelica regularly took her "problem" to Confession. During one session, the priest asked Angelica why she entered cloistered life. "To be a saint," she replied. He told her:

"If you really want to be a saint you should expect somebody hard to live with." To be a saint, he told me, I had to consider my "problem sister" an opportunity to that end. That's when I decided that I would make an effort to be nice to her. It took a lot of sweat and biting of my tongue, but we became good friends.

Not getting along with someone is a two-way street, and many times if one of you is willing to change, the whole relationship can change. I think that's true with any kind of friendship, particularly with negative personalities. Somebody has to get in there and begin the healing. As long as two people are fighting nothing good will happen — and we shouldn't expect the other person to change first. We must look to ourselves. We must endeavor to love those around us, even those we are not instantly disposed to love. Our salvation may depend upon it.

THE GOOD WORK OF YOUR ENEMIES

Do you know why the Lord says "Love your enemies" (Luke 6:27)? Because your enemy does something your friends don't do. Your enemy, which means the person who bugs you, has the power to bring something out in you that is not like Jesus. When your enemy walks into a room, you're already disturbed. It shows that there is something in you that lacks love and gentleness. Don't say, if it wasn't for that person I could be holy. No. You can be holy *because* of that person. That person is making you holy; making you choose the good; making you *like* Jesus.

The actions of your enemy are nothing compared to what you are doing to yourself because of his actions. What's planted in the soil of memory produces fruit, good or bad. Your memory is so filled with anger and hurt feelings that it cannot hold anything good. But if you show mercy and forgiveness toward your enemies, you can blamelessly live in the present, and God will take care of the rest.

FORGIVENESS

Our Lord looked down from the cross and His eyes fell upon the Romans who crucified Him, the Pharisees and Sadducees, the doctors of the law who condemned Him. He didn't see any of His apostles except John. He worked with them for three years. There was His mother and an ex-prostitute. That's all He had.

For coming down from heaven, for thirty years of prayer and work, for three years of healings, miracles, exorcising people from the enemy, for giving sight to the blind and hearing to the deaf, for feeding the multitudes, He is crucified. And what does He say? "Father forgive them, they know not what they do" (Luke 23:34).

Can we say that? Can you honestly say that about the person who did you in, who slighted you, who wronged you? We have to, because He did.

VALLEY DUTY

Some of you have never — if you are really honest with yourself — never loved God as much as you do now. You've never prayed as much as you do now, because you are in trouble, because God has permitted these things in your life. Know that God has not deserted you and that He loves you very much.

In this moment, Jesus asks you to imitate Him as He imitated His Father. He said in the Garden of Gethsemane, "Look Father, You can change all of this. We can do this another way. Nonetheless, not as I will, but as You will." When God asks you to go on "valley duty," when he invites you into the Garden of Gethsemane, know — know that Jesus is in your heart. He is before you and behind you.

TRUST DURING TRIALS

Joseph in the Old Testament had a tremendous amount of trust in God. He is removed from his family, gets a job with Pharaoh, then he lands in jail for years! God finally gets him out by sending Pharaoh a dream.

Look at all the trust Joseph had, all the waiting and not knowing. We have got to learn from this. Don't be discouraged at those times when you question, when you doubt, when you don't understand. There is a darkness in faith. There is that uncertainty, an insecurity in trusting God. Yet, He demands that we believe without seeing; we don't know why things are happening and we certainly don't know what's going to happen. But you must know that the darkness you experience and the anxiety you experience are not a lack of trust; they're part of trust. You've got to let yourself go and persevere in faith.

THE TRIAL OF HANDICAPS

Try to understand that your faith is being put to the test, whatever suffering you have. I dedicated my back brace to the Father, my right leg brace to the Son, and the left leg brace to the Holy Spirit. I told Our Lady, "I'm sorry, no braces for you."

We have to understand the value of suffering. Don't focus on the pain, even as you endure it. One of the great things about Christianity is its honesty. You're going to feel pain. When Jesus was fastened to that cross, unable to move, He felt pain too. If there was any other way to redeem you but this way, He would have done it. Now we must all follow.

THE BEST THING THAT EVER HAPPENED

The man who made my braces had one leg, and there was a brace on it. He said it was the best thing that ever happened to him. He took something tragic and turned it around and made it beautiful. That is what Christians are supposed to do. To give it all to the Lord and unite it to Him with serenity; to not be possessed by anger or resentment.

Prayer in Darkness

"Lord, I'm wounded. I don't know where to go. I don't know what to say. I can't even pray." That may be the best prayer in the world because it demonstrates faith amid darkness.

Mother on Adultery

A woman came to me one time and told me her son had caught her husband with another woman — in adultery.

I said, "What did you tell your husband?"

She said, "He quoted Scripture."

"What did he quote, 'Seek and you shall find'?" I asked.

She said, "No, he quoted what Jesus told the woman taken in adultery. He looked at me and said: 'There is no one to condemn thee woman, neither shall I.' "

So I told her, "Go back and tell him he put the period in the wrong place. Jesus then said: 'Go, and sin no more!' "

Your Personal Cross

We all have crosses, and some we make ourselves. But all of us have a personal cross from God Himself, designed specifically for us. That cross, whether it is physical, mental, spiritual, whatever it is, that particular cross is the main reason why you will be holy and it indicates your glory in heaven. Your entire glory in heaven will be dependent on how you carried your cross.

We waste a lot of time trying to determine whether our cross is from our neighbor or from the Lord, or from ourselves — what difference does it make? If you've got it, carry it. It's to make you holy.

St. Paul says the Leader had to suffer everything in order to teach us. Isn't it strange that He didn't teach us about joy, or health, or happiness? What did He have to teach us? How to suffer — and yet you have people today who run as far from suffering as they can, as if it were evil.

The Brief Trial of Ugly Music

A lot of these satanic groups on the radio sing the same thing over and over. The whole world is now accustomed to this ugly music. Sometimes when I'm waiting at a red light, people will turn their radios up, just to get my goat. It's so ugly, I just ignore it.

A doctor told me, ten years from now they'll all be deaf. I said, thank God for that cross, because then at least the rest of us will have some peace.

AGAINST THE WALL

Sometimes God forces you up against the wall. Don't be discouraged if faith is, at times, difficult and dark for you. Our Lord told the apostles over and over, "It is I, be not afraid. It is I, be not afraid" (John 6:20). When your faith sometimes wavers, and you question, and you're scared; whether that faith requires you to do something or entrust someone to His care; when things seem lost: trust. Sometimes we have to get very low before God will bring us up again.

THE PRAYER OF JUDITH

In 1989 Mother Angelica distributed a copy of the following prayer to her nuns and advised them to recite it daily. It is a prayer for one facing obstacles, persecutions, and adversities. The prayer of Judith is from the Old Testament (Judith 9:5–14), though this version has been "changed a little . . . but not that much" by Mother to suit the needs of her monastery. It is the prayer of a warrior, containing all the gusto and fire that one would expect a prayer favored by Mother Angelica to possess.

At the time, Mother was trying to raise a shortwave radio network in Rome and struggling to keep her television network solvent in the United States. When she shared this with her sisters she called it "a perfect prayer."

O my God, hear me. It is You who were the author of past events, and of what preceded and followed them. The present and the future You have planned. Whatever You devise comes into being; the things You decide upon come forward and say, "Here we are!" All Your ways are in readiness, and Your judgment is made with foreknowledge. Here is a vast force, filled with pride and boasting of their power, trusting in themselves. They do not know that You, the Lord, crush warfare; Lord is Your name.

Shatter their strength in Your might, and crush their force in Your wrath; for they have resolved to profane Your work, to defile the Church where Your glorious name resides; to overthrow

Your altar. See their pride, and send forth Your wrath upon their heads. Strengthen me, O God. Crush their pride with Your hands.

Your strength is not in numbers, nor does Your power depend upon men; but You are the God of the lowly, the Helper of the oppressed, the Supporter of the weak, the Protector of the forsaken, and the Savior of those without hope.

Please, please, God and Lord of Heaven and Earth, Creator of the waters, King of all You have created, hear my prayer! Bring confusion on those who have planned dire things against Your covenant, Your holy temple, and the homes Your children have inherited. Let the whole world know clearly that You are the God of all power and might, and that there is no other who protects us but You alone. Amen.

THE NECESSITY OF TRIALS

If everything had gone smoothly, just as you envisioned, wouldn't you have become very complacent? Would you have depended on the Lord so much? Would you really have known that He's the one doing it all? You might think you could have done without those setbacks and problems and persecutions — but you're wrong. You needed them.

THE LOVE OF JESUS

The Love of Jesus is so strong. It doesn't take away all of your sorrows and trials, but it gives you the endurance and courage to have joy in the midst of them.

AFTER A TRIAL

From 1989 to 1990, Mother Angelica was hard at work trying to establish a shortwave radio network in Rome. Local bureaucracy, financial woes, ecclesial interference, and difficulties with the male religious order she founded, severely tried her during this period. She eventually decided to forgo the Roman plans and build her shortwave operation in Alabama. The following comes from late 1990, just as an array of trials subsided for Angelica. "I feel like an eighteen-wheeler has been removed from my shoulders," she told her nuns at the time. Then she added this reflection:

After a trial, after being under stress for a couple of months (or longer), your faith, and hope, and love, and trust are tested to a point where you scarcely feel religious at all. But when it goes, a trial like that can be like confession: you feel cleansed. You know that God worked in spite of you. You are reminded that when all is said and done, you did nothing, God did everything. Hopefully you can look back on your trials and say, "That was a good thing." I think trials are sent to disable the mechanism of self-reliance that we create for ourselves.

I think the effort of going on, in spite of failures, in spite of setbacks, in spite of the darkness of the night — just plugging along is what God asks of us. The success is not ours at all, only the effort.

10
SIN AND TEMPTATION

Sin is one of those dirty little words one rarely hears today; all choices are equal, and temptation is a nearly forgotten concept. Not to Mother Angelica, however. She never tired of reminding her "family" that evil was alive and well, and as seductive as ever. While she warned of evil's allures and the terrible consequences of sin, she was also quick to point out the limitless mercy of God and the wonder of redemption.

Restoration often begins with awareness, and in the spiritual life, one must know good to recognize its antithesis. Mother's words can help in this regard. They have a convicting quality that will no doubt affect you.

THE GREATEST TEMPTATION

The greatest temptation in the world today repeats what the enemy once said to Eve: "Why don't you try it? It isn't true that you will die. How are you going to know if you don't try it once? How are you going to know good from evil if all you've ever known is good?" That is the oldest temptation in the world; and it works in every century, in every soul, as if it were a brand-new trick.

THE SLAVERY OF SIN

We think of slavery as being subject to someone else. But the core of slavery is the loss of personal freedom. I can't do as I please. I'm hampered, diminished, and domineered. However, there is a slavery worse than that.

When we become slaves to ourselves, then we are slaves indeed. When you come to a point in your life where you cannot say no to your own desires, you are indeed a slave. Even a person in a concentration camp is still free in his mind. But when your imagination, or memory, makes demands upon you, and your will is so weak that it offers no resistance, then you are in a moral quicksand. Your will goes wherever the imagination sends it, and that is the worst kind of slavery. It is the slavery of a soul captive within itself.

THE STINK OF SIN

Sin has a way of sticking to us. When I would return home after a day out, my habit smelled like tobacco. I never smoked in my life. But that is the world: it stinks and it clings to you. Pretty soon you don't smell it anymore. That's the way habitual sin, serious sin is. We cannot get in the Presence of God forever smelling like that. That is the purpose of suffering, to remove the smell.

POPOVER CHRISTIANS

We have a lot of popover Christians. You know what a popover is? That's those things you put in the toaster and, ploop!, they flip. Well, some Christians are like that. They vacillate between good and evil. They are a scandal. They resemble the light, but they can't convey it, because as soon as they move toward holiness, they pop over to the other side and lose what little they have gained.

Some of you claim to be with God, and the minute the devil and flesh come to call you pop over — after all, God's merciful, right?

I want to ask you a question: What happens if your little ticker stops and you're popped over on the wrong side? You know what you are? Presumptuous. You are presuming that God's Infinite Mercy will save you. Well don't forget about His Infinite Justice.

Playing with Temptation

You know, if you are bit by a chained dog, you can't blame the dog. If you put yourself in temptation and you fall you cannot blame anyone but yourself. The devil has been chained, but when you go live in his pen, you are risking eternity. The grace and the Precious Blood of Jesus have penned him up. But when you give your mind, and heart, and will over to temptation, the teeth marks are on your soul.

The Strategy of the Enemy

The devil may not get your soul, but he will use every means possible to decrease your degree of glory in the kingdom. He will watch, and wait, and determine your weakest point, and then he will work on that. This is the strategy of the enemy.

We are in a battle, and when you are in a battle you have to have at least a suspicion about where your enemy is going next.

Selling Out for Peanuts

In late 1967, ever the entrepreneur, Mother Angelica was on the lookout for a new venture to pay down the debt of her Birmingham monastery. The fishing lure business that had financed the property had literally gone south by that point.

Introduced to peanut roasting by a friend, Mother felt inspired, and the Li'l Ole Peanut Company was born the following week in a monastery workroom. For almost five years, the nuns of Our Lady of the Angels churned out roasted peanuts and turned a healthy profit, until Mother's conscience was violated.

We used to roast peanuts at the monastery. We did five tons a month and had big concessions. Our concessionaire changed and the new guy came to me and said, "Mother, I would love to continue giving you the peanut concession."

I said, "Fine."

Then he said, "Of course, there will be a small fee."

"Like what?" I said.

He said, "Well, you know, an advertising fee."

"How much?" I asked.

"About $1,000 dollars a year."

I said, "That's a kickback." He looked at

me like he didn't think nuns knew that. He must have thought all nuns were idiots. Don't go by appearances, because I'm from an Italian family. My grandpa had a saloon. So I said, "That is a kickback and I don't pay kickbacks."

"You lose me and you're as good as out of business," he said.

"That's okay. I don't need it. Look buddy, if I'm going to hell, it's not going to be on account of a peanut!" I said.

What's the peanut in your life? We all begin by silencing our conscience, looking the other way, putting aside this principle or that. And one day you look back and you've sold your soul for a peanut. Doesn't matter what it is, it's all peanuts compared to the value of your soul.

A Slow Fall

All falls are gradual. Man is not like a stone rolling downhill. Man falls very slowly — almost unconsciously. He slips gradually, over a long period of time. *We are creatures of habit, and if we have acquired a habit of goodness, it is difficult to fall quickly.* The fall usually comes bit by bit. It's like daily prayer.

Things crowd in on you, so you cut it

short. The next day something else comes up. The next day you skip it. You keep this up for days, and weeks, and months, and the first thing you know you have stopped praying altogether. It has been so gradual, and now you have so many things to do, and so many places to go, prayer is a torture. If it isn't practiced regularly, sanctity can slip away in the same fashion.

THE COMMUNAL ASPECT OF SIN

No one sins without offending heaven and earth. Remember the prodigal son said, "I have sinned against heaven and against earth and against you" (Luke 15:21). So there is a communal aspect of sin, and a communal aspect of holiness.

LUCIFER'S PRIDE

The angels had a problem with pride. That's where Lucifer went astray. He attributed all the gifts God gave him to himself. And so, as a result, no one could be greater than him. He didn't particularly mind that the Most High was above him, but no one else could be next to the Most High. To find out that human beings, a man and a woman, would be above him was more than he could take. So he said, "I will not serve."

210

This is happening today. Pride of the intellect, pride of will, and pride of spiritual gifts are everywhere.

JESUS AND THE SIN OF PRIDE

In the Gospel, Our Lord is very lenient on those who have moral failings. You have the woman taken in adultery, the prostitute, the thieves, the tax collectors — pretty big sinners. Jesus had great compassion for these people. They all suffered from sins of weakness, physical and emotional weakness.

The sin of pride is a different matter. He seemed to have no compassion for the Pharisees. When we arrive at that great pride that says, "I will not serve," we have essentially denied the existence of God. It can lead to very deeply rooted sins. Though God works on these people all the time, they can die in their sins because they don't have anybody above them, except possibly themselves.

THE IMAGINATION OF JUDAS

You know the strange thing about Judas? The Scripture tells us that during the Last Supper, when the Lord gave him a morsel of bread and said, "What you are going to do, do quickly," Judas decided, at that moment, to betray his Master (John 13:27–30). It was then that the devil entered into him. But up until that moment, Judas was entertaining thoughts of blasphemy against his Master. This man wasn't the type of leader Judas wanted; he wanted a military leader. So for two or three years he entertained thoughts of greed, he kept them in his mind, his imagination began to work overtime. His memory began to bring out things in the Master's life that he didn't like. So these two faculties in Judas, his memory and his imagination, were being utilized in bad ways.

You know, in your own mind you can have a party, a movie; your mind can be a whole house of good or bad fantasies. The Master said that the enemy was "the father of lies" and "when he lies he is drawing on his own store" (John 8:44). Your mind is a store.

We are fighting visible foes, and invisible ones. How do we fight them — foes that instill thoughts into the minds of men, women, and children? You can fight with love. You can fight by giving your heart and soul to God. You can fight by controlling your imagination and memory, by not harboring resentments; by being hurt, but not hurting in return; by avoiding occasions of sin, and people who try to lead you to sin. Many a mind needs a house cleaning. They are cluttered up with ambitions, filth, and evil. We may be weak, but we have within us the Spirit of the Lord God, and we must call on the Spirit to help us control our imaginations, and fill them with the things of God.

COMEDY AND TRAGEDY

Try to laugh a lot, because life is funny and everybody today is too serious. The only tragedy in the world, my friend, is sin.

THE TEMPTATION TO DESPAIR

Any temptation to despair is not of God, and you need to remember that the enemy wants you to despair. Know your enemy. He's not handing you roses, he's handing you hell. So be careful of any kind of despair. Those temptations come directly from the liar, the enemy who was a liar from the beginning. He cannot give truth. He cannot give beauty. He can't give you anything that is good. He wants to take that good away from you. The only thing he can do to a human being is to encourage him to despair — what a waste of time it is to listen to a liar. Listen to the Lord, pray for the grace to overcome the temptation, and keep moving.

SPIRITUAL VALLEYS

Every soul in the world is tempted to sadness. We call it the noonday devil. You know, so many people talk about Blue Monday — you've had a good weekend then here comes Monday! Wash day, kids, lunches, work, and the same old thing over again. The very fact that you had to shake yourself out of some kind of relaxation brings on feelings of sadness. This is a valley.

But why should a Christian ever have a valley? Why do life's problems cause such deep valleys in our lives, which we can't escape? Why do anger and resentments dig such deep valleys in our memories? Have we no concept of God as Father? Are we under the impression that these horrible things are happening to us and He doesn't know it? If it is happening, it has either been permitted by God or ordained by Him. He will not interfere with free will, so He does permit evil. But we should not let someone else's evil action dig a valley into our souls and push God out. Only we can do that.

We cannot blame anyone or anything for the deep valleys in our lives. We want to put blame on other people and things because it excuses us. Our Dear Lord didn't do that. On the day He was crucified He didn't blame anyone. He said, "Father forgive them, they know not what they do" (Luke 23:34). He died with no valleys in his soul, no crevices where resentment, and hatred, or anger, or self-pity could hide and warp and disfigure the soul.

An Ocean of Mercy

I was on the beach in California years ago. And I like to call the waves to me when I stand at the seashore. Everybody thinks I'm nuts, but I figure they belong to my Father, so if I want to call them in, I can call them in. I try to get them to touch my shoes.

So I'm there in the sand saying, "Come on! Come on! You can do it!" Well, this great big wave came in. It came up past my ankles. My shoes were wet. My brace was full of sand. As I stood there, a drop from the ocean hit my hand and I looked at it. Then I looked out at the vast sea. At that moment the Lord said to me, "Angelica, that drop represents all your sins, all your imperfections, and all your frailties. Throw it in the ocean." So I threw it back. And then the Lord said, "The ocean is My mercy. Now if you looked for that drop, would you ever find it?"

I said, "No, Lord."

You see, your sins are like that drop in the ocean. Every day, every minute of the day, throw your drop in the ocean of His mercy. Then don't worry, just try harder.

GONE WITH THE WIND

I realized after many years that I had to be just plain me, with my impatience that I have worked on for so many years, with my anger.

You know, I separate Church and State real fast when somebody tries to cheat me. One time I told the electric company off so badly . . . Three years later I went to give a talk at a Methodist church and a man from the church came to pick me up. And we're driving along, and he says, "You don't remember me?" I said, "No." He said, "I remember you. I work for the electric company." Phew!

I struggle with the past, thinking there are times I should have done things differently, but didn't. I give those moments to the Lord. He knows it all. The past is like a bubble; a little bit of wind and it's gone. Once you have asked the Lord for forgiveness, the wind of the Holy Spirit blows through the past and all your mistakes are gone. So accept the Lord's mercy and let them go.

Confession vs. Burning

In the United States, and in other parts of the world, there has developed a recent "tradition" of committing one's sins to paper and burning them in a public ceremony. The practice, in some communities, has replaced private confession. It is a "tradition" that Mother Angelica had little patience for.

Let me tell you something, sweetheart, writing your sins on a piece of paper and having somebody burn them does not take them away. That's the biggest fallacy there could be. What you're saying is, "If I put my sins down and burn them, that's absolution." No, that is a farce. Don't depend on that. If you have a sin on your soul, then you should have the privilege of going to Confession. It's a healing sacrament. You just don't get rid of something, you need healing also, and you get the grace to be stronger the next time you face temptation.

Get Thee to a Confessional

Do something nice for your neighbor this week. Go to Confession. Make a good confession. When you come out and say your penance, you're as pure as an angel. Not only are you forgiven every single sin — if you died at that minute you'd go straight to heaven! What's wrong with you? Don't just sit there and ho-hum. You're ho-humming yourself into purgatory!

THE TRUTH ABOUT CONFESSION

I think a lot of people believe that God has a huge book up there and He keeps adding your sins to it. When you go to Confession, it's gone. Our Dear Lord forgives and forgets. I think it was St. Margaret Mary Alacoque whose confessor did not believe that Our Lord appeared to her. So he said to her, "I want proof. You tell the Lord that He should tell you what my last grievous sin was. If He tells you, then I will believe you."

So she went back to Confession and the priest inquired, "Have you asked the Lord?" "Yes," she said. "What did He say?" St. Margaret Mary answered, "The Lord said, 'Tell your confessor, I don't remember.' " Boy, the Lord humiliated that priest. Like your confessor, God forgets your sins.

Jesus paid the price of Original Sin, but that does not mean that you can sin all you want — that's presumption. God did not die for you to sin more. He died that you might not sin at all. He merited grace for you and opened the gates of heaven for you.

You and Me

You are a holy bunch of sinners, and I'm in the club too.

Human Nature

Your human nature, as weak as it is, is part of sanctity. God is calling you and me to great heights of holiness, with our human nature. He does not intend for us to destroy it; He intends for us to conquer it!

Prayer for Inner Healing

Lord God, Father of all, we come before Thee today empty with our soul in need of healing. We need that confidence and hope that comes from Your Holy Spirit. Help us to realize Your love for us and to give that love to our neighbor. We need to build and renew. There is in each of us something in our memory that keeps us from being compassionate and merciful. So deeply rooted are these gnawing resentments that they obstruct us from the good You have for us. We ask You to reach into each of our memories now and heal them. Touch that unforgiving spirit within us and drive it away, Father. We know You forgive us, but we find it so hard to forgive ourselves. Remove all the regrets of the past. Lord Father, we know You are present now and beg You to remove all of our guilt and make us new so we can be used by Your Son. Lord Father, reach in and heal us all and fill us with the love and compassion that surpass all understanding. Amen.

11
SAINTS AND ANGELS

We are all called to be saints. This simple message was at the heart of Mother Angelica's public preaching, and became the goal of all she did. She was trying to help people achieve sanctity.

Mother is perhaps the first media personality to make the saints, the apostles, and the great biblical characters fully human and accessible. In her talks, she exploited their flaws and failings to help us see ourselves in their journeys. Suddenly, sainthood didn't seem such a remote destination. Here are some of her choice insights on the saints, as well as a few reflections on angels and their importance in our lives. One would expect the woman who founded Our Lady of the Angels Monastery to have a few thoughts on these heavenly messengers.

A GREAT SAINT

A saint is one who empties himself and takes on the image of Jesus, so that the person and Jesus are look-alikes.

We should not aim to be a great saint for the purpose of being a great saint. A saint is the last to admit or know that he is a saint. A saint's goal is to get as close to God as he can, not for his own sake, but for His sake. The aim is to give honor and glory to God, and to totally forget the self.

BEING A SAINT

Being a saint is being who you were meant to be: a frail human being keeping the Commandments, especially the new one. It's loving when you are not loved in return. It's being patient when you want to hit somebody on the head. It's loving your family as they are, not as you want them to be. It's not letting the disappointments in your life crush you. The challenge of Christianity is to have fortitude in times of suffering; to stand for the truth, even if you stand alone; to be undeterred by obstacles; to know that there is a big world out there and you are a weak, little person. But God is looking for weakness so His power can be manifest — He needs you!

A Saint Loves

A saint is someone who loves God above all things and loves his neighbor with that same love — with a holy love, a deep love, a persevering love.

The Canonized and Uncanonized Varieties

Canonization is nothing more than the Church saying publicly that they know for sure that this person is in heaven. I mean, there are millions of people in heaven who are not canonized. That's why we have All Saints' Day . . .

I always thought, personally, that the saints who are canonized may be the very least in the kingdom. We don't know that, but it's a good guess. Some little old washerwoman who had tremendous love for God may be greater than St. Augustine up there. I think we're going to have lots of little surprises when we arrive.

Seeing Lasting Reality

What is the difference between a saint and a good person? I think this is the missing link: there must be a perfect harmony between the visible and invisible. I must see the visible, and at the same time see the invisible reality in it, with the eyes of my soul. What I see with my physical eyes will eventually disappear, including myself.

SAVORING THE ROSES

St. Francis de Sales one day was looking at a rose, and he put his hands to his ears and he said to the rose, "Stop shouting." There is a power in the love of God. Most people today look at a rose and they don't see anything; only a name, a color, a fragrance. But these great saints saw God in everything.

BIOGRAPHERS IN PURGATORY

When I began work on Mother Angelica's biography she wished me forty years in purgatory if I dared "sugarcoat" her life. I think I dodged the bullet. This following excerpt helps explain why she was so adamant:

I like to sit in bed, eating bon-bons, and reading the mortified lives of the saints. When I was a young novice I used to flip through those biographies looking for someone like me.

I need nine hours of sleep a day. The medication I take requires me to eat seven times a day. I like air conditioning and comfortable chairs. I went through all the lives of the saints and I couldn't find one like me.

But I came to the conclusion that the saints weren't the problem, it was their biographers. I've often said that I wish every biographer of every saint, who did not depict the truth, would go to purgatory for forty years, because they have made the saints unreal. You'd swear these people were holy when they were conceived, after reading one of these accounts. But it's not true. The saints would be the first to tell you: they struggled like you do. They ate, and drank, and slept, and were frustrated, and victims of injustice. They were like you! Can you imagine emptying heaven now and putting all the saints in a big arena? They would look just like you do now: fat and skinny, young and old. They had their faults and eccentricities. They bugged people. It takes a saint to live with one. Every Christian is supposed to bug somebody. That's what the saints did.

No Quick Path to Sainthood

One of the problems with reading the lives of the saints is that you're reading about people who have achieved a high degree of union with God. Rarely included are the multitudinous rises and falls they experienced; or the time it took them to get to that place of union. They never write about the struggle, they always write about the end result. So don't imagine that you can be a saint lickety-split. You have to go through the process, and that could take a lifetime.

THE PATRON SAINT OF THE GROUCHY

Did you ever see a statue of a grouchy saint? I saw one once. It was the most gorgeous statue I ever saw. It was Padre Pio, who was a grouch, you know. Now, everybody excuses the poor guy and says, "Well, he had the stigmata and he was suffering." Come off it. He was a grouch; he was a typical Italian grouch — which I can relate to! So I bought that statue in New Orleans a few years ago. He has the most beautiful, grumpy look on his face. See, that's my kind of saint. I want a saint who struggles like I do. There's no such thing as perfection. There is only the struggle for holiness.

THE IMPERFECTION OF THE SAINTS

Our saints had faults. There's only one Immaculate Conception and there ain't any others.

Look at Padre Pio. He was noted for his gruffness, which God used. One time these two obnoxious, old, Italian women were arguing — pushing each other at the Communion rail, each trying to get the Host from Padre Pio before the other one. Well, he just passed them both by. And they're yelling and screaming. So Padre Pio came back and just let them have it, corrected them right then and there, during Communion! He got impatient. But don't excuse your saints. They're imperfect many times, just like you. What they have, that we lack, is that determination to be holy.

FAT AND HOLY

Society tells us we are a product of our environment, our background, and I suppose we are in a way. But I think this sometimes keeps us from holiness. St. Francis Borgia came out of one of the most rotten families in Italy: the Borgias. His great-grandfather was Pope Alexander VI, an evil man.

Francis is a great consolation to me. First of all, he was big and fat, and I have a little weight problem. Francis Borgia was so fat they had to cut a hole in the table so he could reach his food. St. Thomas Aquinas was also rotund. He would get nervous and all he did was eat, eat, eat. And don't believe those skinny statues of St. Anthony you've seen. He was no slim Jim either. He was fat, real fat.

I love to pick the saints apart, but I fear there'll have to be a solitary confinement in heaven, just for me. I've been telling the truth about the saints for so many years, nobody will want to talk to me when I get up there.

St. Anthony: Big and Bold

St. Anthony was four foot eleven, fat, and had dropsy — I think he just ate too much. St. Anthony was so holy that he went to a village where no one would listen to him and he wandered over to the beach. He called forth every kind of fish to listen to him, and every type of fish came forward. Scared the death out of those villagers.

Tempted Saints

Blessed Matt Talbot was an alcoholic in the early 1900s. He used to tie his hands to the bed at night with chains so he wouldn't go out and drink. St. Francis de Sales had a terrible temper. He almost committed suicide one time when he got the temptation that he was damned. He went to bed for two weeks. Finally the thought came to him, "Even if I were damned, I can love God now," and the temptation was gone. St. Ignatius had a terrible time with temptations. The saints were people like you. They had to fight for sanctity where they were.

THE IMPETUOUS LOVE OF ST. FRANCIS

One time St. Francis and Brother Masseo arrived at a fork in the road. Brother Masseo asked Francis which road they should take. Francis said, "Brother, spin like a top, and when you fall from being dizzy we will go in whatever direction you are facing." Can you imagine that man saying "okay"? But he loved St. Francis so much he would have stood on his head in a creek for him. So he spins around and falls and they went in the direction he was facing.

Now today we look at that and think: "This is kind of wacko." But it's not wacko, because the saints are not like the rest of us, who are so proper. They're people in love, and they couldn't care less about human respect. People in love do crazy things. Love doesn't think. Love acts, then thinks. Most people think, and then act, but lovers don't do that. They're impetuous. St. Francis was so in love with God that he wanted everything he did to depend on the Providence of God — even the choice of which road to take. How often do we rely on His Providence?

EMPTYING YOURSELF FOR HOLINESS

There was a wolf in this little village that would go out at night and attack people. The villagers told St. Francis how frightened they were. So one night he goes out and the fearsome wolf is snarling and growling at him, and Francis says, "Peace, brother." Well, that wolf crawled right to the ground. Francis told the wolf that he had done terrible things. "But if you're very nice," he said, "the people will feed you. Now, I don't want to hear another thing from you."

The wolf grew very gentle, the people fed him, and he lived to a ripe old age. Now, you say, how does that make you holy? It doesn't. Francis was holy first, then the power of God moved through him and he was able to do wonderful things. See, it isn't who you are or who I am that counts. It's who He is, and how much room we make for Him to do the things He desires with us. It's a matter of emptying yourself and letting Jesus work through you. If you do that, He may just be able to tame the wolf inside of you.

MEDITATION ON ST. PETER

I love to think of St. Peter coming into the gates of Rome one day, probably barefoot and carrying his shoes. He had absolutely nothing but the grace of God. Who knew then that that man would change the world? You think the Roman senators knew? Or the wealthy? Roman society's leading lights?

He was a man so holy that his shadow healed (Acts 5:15). Can you imagine a shadow healing? He was a big, blustery fisherman — just like you, without the fish. He was a man who always spoke before he thought. He was convinced he could do everything better than everybody else, then he forgot to do it. Peter should give us great hope.

ST. FRANCIS'S STRUGGLE FOR CHASTITY

Holy Father Francis had great temptations against chastity, so he went out and made three snowmen. He said, "Now, Francis, this is your wife and these are your children." It didn't help. So you know what he did? The next time he had a temptation it happened to be spring (the next reported temptation anyway). So he went out and rolled himself in a rose bush. To this day there are no thorns in that bush — they're all in Francis! He struggled. What makes you better?

The Temper of St. Philip Neri

St. Philip Neri had a terrible temper. He was fastidious, a real neato. The sacristan would deliberately not clean Philip's chalice in the morning. Then Philip would stand there at the altar anguishing over that dirty chalice. One day he went before the Lord and said, "Please, Lord, make me gentle." And he knelt before the Blessed Sacrament for three hours. After all that prayer he felt very gentle and assumed he had "caught" gentleness.

He went out of the chapel and came across a very kind brother with whom he had never had words. But the man just didn't look right — his habit was a mess and Philip blasted him. Then he saw the sacristan who never cleaned his chalice and Philip's blood got to boiling — so he blasted him too. Well, he felt awful. Philip returned to the Tabernacle and promptly blamed the Lord, like we all do. He said, "Didn't I spend three hours in here asking for gentleness? And look what happened!" The Lord said, "Philip, you have asked me for gentleness, and I have multiplied the opportunities in which you can be gentle."

You see, holiness is a sinner that falls and rises. Sinners are those who never rise. So if you're struggling, you're in good shape.

SAINTLY SUFFERING

The saints suffered. Therese had tuberculosis. Teresa of Avila had cancer of the stomach. Padre Pio had perpetual diarrhea and asthma. Bernadette had asthma too. Mother Cabrini had high fever due to malaria she contracted during her travels. Holiness is not for wimps and the cross is not negotiable, sweetheart, it's a requirement.

HOLINESS IS FOR SINNERS

If you are going to be holy, for God's sake, aim for the top. I wouldn't aim to get in the gate. Your faults and weaknesses and sins have absolutely nothing to do with achieving holiness. Many a great sinner became holy. Sometimes it's the goody-goody types that have a harder time, because they are so complacent. They lack the thrust of a sinner, the energy to repair their ways and push ahead in the spiritual life.

CONVERSION: THE ENDLESS BATTLE

You don't have to be old to be a saint. Mary of Egypt was sixteen. She was a prostitute during the crusades. She went with the crusaders to ply her trade, and when they arrived at one of the big basilicas in Jerusalem, she tried to go in with them. She got as far as the door, when an invisible force held her back. There in the courtyard was a statue of the Virgin Mary. So she sat down under a tree, staring at that statue, and said, "Oh, God, I wished my soul looked like that. I am so sorry." She went out into the desert for forty years to do penance for her sins. Bishops and cardinals and kings went out to seek her counsel.

Now, you can imagine that because she had her conversion, she never had another temptation. But you would be wrong. All of us are sinners. Every one of us battles something. An interior conversion is only the beginning. Then you've got to keep fighting for holiness.

CHANGING EACH DAY

I think these are times for great holiness and great saints, greater than any time in the past because there is more evil, more temptation. The fight is greater. The danger is greater and the opportunities are greater. God is not mocked and this world is not going to pot. You can save it. You can change it by being faithful to the duties of your state of life with holiness.

God will raise his saints in this age, and they will change the world. He gives you an opportunity right now to do it, and if you don't it will still be done, by another. Each one of us must look upon the world as our own personal duty to change.

ANGELS

In the very first book of Genesis, the Lord said, "Let there be light," and there was light. Then he created the sun and the moon. Well, I think the first creation was the angels, the angelic nature. It is reasonable that God would create a creature most like Himself, a creature of pure spirit. We are made to the image of God, but our body is in no way like God. Only our soul, our memory, our will is like God. But the angels are creatures of total intellect. Your soul freed from your body will be pure spirit when you die. The angels began their existence in this state.

ANGELS IN SCRIPTURE

When we talk of angels being pure spirits, we are talking about intelligences. Every one is a different species, every one is unique. The angelic nature is different from ours.

Scripture tells us an awful lot about the angelic nature. Now, modern theologians keep saying there are no angels, and I feel sorry for them. We should feel sorry for anyone that lives half a life.

There are times in the Scripture when the Jews, who had such a fear of Yahweh, would not mention His name and would sometimes call Him "an angel." But there are innumerable passages that mark a distinct creation from our own: a creature not God and not human, but purely spiritual. For instance: "I will send my angel before you to guard you in all your ways" (Psa. 91:11). In the book of Tobit, a very interesting book, young Tobias is protected by St. Raphael who identifies himself as one who ever stands before the son of God (Tobit 12:15).

THE NINE CHOIRS

There are nine choirs or groups of angels mentioned in Scripture. The seraphim is the highest, and their only duty is to praise God. Then there are the cherubim and thrones. Those three constitute the first hierarchy. Then you have dominations, virtues, and powers (mentioned by St. Paul in Col. 1:16). These all have specific works to do. They are not just dilly-dallying up there. The third hierarchy is made up of principalities, archangels, and angels. The lowest choir has been given to us as guardians.

THE SERAPHIM

The seraphim are the highest angels. They have a vast amount of intelligence and can acquire tremendous amounts of knowledge very quickly. Their sole purpose for existence is to worship God. The seraphim are all about love. The book of Revelation tells us that they are the ones who keep saying, "Holy, holy, holy, Lord God of Hosts, heaven and earth are full of Your glory" (Rev. 4:8).

GUARDIAN ANGELS

We've all seen that picture of a giant angel and this little bitty kid on the bridge. Do you remember that picture of the guardian angels? Most of you forgot about them after that. The kid grew up and the angel went away. No! That angel has been with you from your conception and will be there at your death. St. Paul says, "There was standing beside me an angel of God to whom I belong and whom I serve" (Acts 27:23). That's a wonderful example of a guardian angel. Why don't you name yours?

237

Most of you don't even talk to him — probably because you didn't name him. What would it hurt you, when you wake up, to have a little conversation with your angel? Say, "Thank you, angel, for watching over me during the night. Pray for me today that I do not offend God." It's a simple thing. Remember your guardian angel sees the face of the Father in heaven. I named mine Fidelis. That means faithful. He has been faithful to me and interceded for me when I didn't know Jesus, prayed for me during my entire vocation, throughout my life as a nun. He guides and guards me every day. I love him.

You Need Your Angel

The Lord Himself said, "Do not scandalize one of these little ones, for their angels in heaven ever see the face of my Father" (Matt. 18:10). Now, we cannot relegate angels to children alone. You are the one who really needs an angel.

Knowing that His archenemy, Satan, who is jealous of your dignity as a Christian and as a son of God, seeks to destroy you, God has given you your own guardian angel. When you compare your intelligence to the intelligence of an angel, it's like comparing a pigmy to Einstein. All the knowledge of the world from this day to the end of time is all within the mind of the smallest angel. Now, when you pit your intelligence against that, you're in trouble. So God has given you an angel to be at your side — ever present, never leaving you, to guard, and protect, and to inspire you. Many of the inspirations you get come from your angel.

The realization that you and I have a being, a friend, a protector that is so magnificent in beauty, should fill us with consolation. You know, if you had a personal friend with a higher intelligence who wanted to be with you, you'd be so tickled. Yet each of us has beside us this magnificent creature, an angel, a spirit of the Lord — and he is with us now. What is so tragic today is that one of the most consoling invisible realities in the whole wide world is hardly known, talked about or cared about. You think you are alone, but that is only an illusion — one of the many illusions we have.

MAKING USE OF YOUR GUARDIAN ANGEL

One of the things we don't take advantage of is the power, the intelligence, the guardianship, the inspirations of our angel. I think in today's world, he is the one that can do the very most for you.

The angels had to face a test, as you and I must. The higher the intelligence, the more necessary the test. God wants to be chosen, He doesn't want to force you to love him. But you have a choice: to forget the Author of our being and His gifts or embrace Him. And throughout Scripture we have glimpses of this test.

They realized that God was going to create an inferior nature, and that the second person of the Trinity would take upon Himself a human nature. The angels would have to submit themselves to this divine human being. The test was one of humility. Would you submit yourself to a dog? What if God said, "Here is a dumb, ugly dog, and I am going to make him superior to you." What would you say? "I'll never serve that creature." This was a tremendous comedown for God. When the angels discovered this, some, like St. Michael, championed the cause. But Lucifer, the brightest star, the most intelligent and beautiful angel, said this is not just, it is not right. He said, "I will not serve. I am the greatest and this Son of God should take upon Himself my nature." Seems logical? Very logical. And Scripture reports that one third of the angels followed him and fell.

THE ROOT OF THEIR FALL AND OURS

Jesus Himself said once, "I saw Lucifer fall from heaven like lightning." You see, the fall of the angels was very sudden because their intelligence is so great. When those angels chose hell it was with perfect knowledge, it was not a surprise. They chose hell rather than serve Jesus made man. The sin of the angels was pride; the sin of Adam and Eve was pride. And your sins and mine, all without exception, stem from pride. There are prostitutes and thieves, murderers and addicts in the kingdom, but there are no proud people in the kingdom — not even one.

The Phantom COMIC STRIP

Some mornings I lie in bed and read *The Phantom,* which is my little comic strip of choice. One of my sisters says, "I just can't believe that you read *The Phantom* every week." Well, let me tell you about that cartoon. To me it's a struggle between good and evil. Last week the Phantom was in an impossible situation. He's trapped in a prison and his enemies are hanging all over him and there's a rope around his neck; they've got him in a stranglehold. I like it because he's always getting into these impossible situations. I think, "How's he going to get out of this one?" So all of a sudden this dog breaks in and releases him from the clutches of his enemies.

It's such an example for me. I know you all think I'm a little bit wacko, but what happens in those situations in our lives when we seem to be caught in a stranglehold? That dog, to me, is like the angels who are sent by God to save us: Michael, and all his cohorts who come to release us from bondage. Then we are free to overcome our weak will, our faults or dryness, our physical pain. We get into bondage at times, and the only ones that can help us are the Lord and His angels.

Tough Angels

Angels could kill 260,000 people in one night. One angel went through Egypt and killed the firstborn humans, cows, sheep, dogs, cats, locusts — everything that was firstborn went. That angel was powerful.

Poor St. Frances of Rome. Her angel would knock her down every time she committed a fault. You mustn't think that the angels are these plump, gentle beings. They are strong. If I were St. Frances I would have just stayed on the floor and said, "I'll be down here." The angel would literally knock her over. Maybe that's what we need.

A Lesson in Prayer

The angels surround you and never take their eyes away from the Father in heaven. Wonder of wonders, they are not distracted from God or from their duty to care for you. What a lesson in perfect prayer they are.

12
EMBRACING
INSPIRATION AND RISK

If a fifty-eight-year-old, crippled, cloistered nun with only a high school education could create a media empire with little more than faith and guts, what excuse do you really have? Mother Angelica's willingness to obey the slightest inspiration, and her stunning capacity for risk, all but ensured her incredible success. There is much to learn from her example.

Mother is a woman possessed by inspiration and doggedly determined to fulfill God's will, no matter the cost. How did she discern and process her inspirations? Where did she find the strength to move forward in the face of such impossible odds? And why did she risk so much, while fearing so little? A few answers follow.

This section is designed for all those who have heard that "still small voice" calling them to do something, something big and bold, but have yet to act. It is for all of us who have felt called to a "ridiculous" work and hesitated. Heed Mother Angelica's words and mark them well. They are not the honeyed pabulum of motivational gurus, or seven keys to this or that, but the practical wisdom of one who built a worldwide network with only the assistance of God. Here is how she did what she did . . .

INSPIRATIONS

Once I get an inspiration, I never question it. I know myself, and I believe if God wants it, He has His plan. *If you are following God, He never shows you the end. It's always a walk of faith.* Franciscan virtue is to follow the Providence of God, and God's Providence goes as far as you go. Now that's the scary thing about it. If you don't go, He won't go.

For instance, take the monastery and buildings. We were told it would cost five to six million dollars. All of a sudden along comes a million-dollar donation. Now I know God a little bit, not a lot, but a little bit, and when he gives you a million dollars He means for you to start. I could have put it in the bank and waited for the other four or five million, but that would have shown an immediate distrust in His Providence. Did I know the rest was coming? No. But once I feel something is from God, I start out with a sincere heart and mind. Even if I have a doubt about something, I just keep at it. Then God begins to show Himself.

DISCERNING INSPIRATIONS

It's very hard to discern what is of the Lord in our inspirations and what is of our selves. There are times when there is no question. But those times are few and far between. More often we need to listen attentively to the Lord and always be prepared to answer yes.

FEAR FROM PRIDE

The task that God gives us, the mission, the apostolate, is to keep ourselves open to the Spirit; and that's so hard, owing to our fears. Pride is the thing that makes us afraid. Whenever we fear, it is always pride. It means at that point we have begun to have confidence in ourselves or other people. And once you do that, your nature knows you can't do it, and distrust of others soon follows.

WILD IDEAS

In the eyes of God, we're all children. He said, "Unless you become like little children

you shall not enter the kingdom of heaven"
(Matt. 18:3). That means you must have
the love, the confidence, the boldness of a
child. Loving children have wild imaginings
and wild ideas. They promise to build their
parents castles when they grow up, and to
someday bring love to the whole world. You
can never have wild ideas when it comes to
God. He accepts even the wildest plans,
knowing there's no way for you to fulfill
them. But He can.

GROWING COLD IN SUCCESS

When you make a goal for yourself that you
can arrive at, you lose because you are no
longer willing to sacrifice or to put up with
the sacrifices of daily living. When the goal
is far off, we are struggling and living on
the level of faith. But when we have arrived,
we begin to live on the level of memory and
imagination — where the only thing that
matters is the satisfaction of our own desires, a state of self-indulgence. We no longer
live on the level of faith, and everything
begins to fall apart.

For example, when you are struggling, you
are more dependent on God. Many people
will say they were closer to God when they
were struggling than they are now that they
are successful. Because you wanted some-

thing and you knew that it was not within your reach, so you were more reliant on God — you put forth more effort, and you prayed more. You were more selfless and did not have time to live on an emotional level. But now that you have arrived and felt the glamour of success, the glamorous feelings of satisfaction and having everything at your fingertips, you depart from faith and focus on what you want. Self-satisfaction becomes the focus, and we grow independent of God. We must thank God for every success because He bears the fruit, we merely spread the seeds.

PUTTING A LID ON GOD

Never put a lid on God. You can't give God a thimble and ask for a quart. It won't work. Your plans, your projects, your dreams have to always be bigger than you, so God has room to operate. I want you to get good ideas, crazy ideas, extravagant ideas. Nothing is too much for The Lord to do — accent on "The Lord."

TOTAL DEPENDENCE

I must prefer the love of Jesus to everything and everybody, and that's where you have to put forth mental discipline. Even if I know I'm not doing something well, or lack the time to do it well, then I have to ask Jesus for His help. We have to arrive at that total dependence upon the Lord, and it's so difficult because we always want to do something on our own.

MOTHER'S DEFINITION OF FAITH

Faith is one foot on the ground, one foot in the air, and a queasy feeling in the stomach. You don't know what's going to happen tomorrow, but you do know that His Presence and His Providence rise before the dawn, and that's all you need to know.

NO RETICENCE

Never hamper God's work in you by questioning His designs in your life. Be free to fly into His arms without any barrier.

FEAR OF FAILURE

Even after healing and performing miracles, Jesus couldn't get twelve friends to stick by Him. He wasn't afraid of failure. He took failure to the very end, so that you may rise above it. You can't disappoint Him. Just do what He asks of you right now.

If you have God with you, you do not need assurance. You need zeal.

You Can Do All Things

We must be unafraid of ridicule or human respect, unafraid to walk out alone, knowing that we are nothing and can do nothing on our own. But with His grace and His power you can do all things.

Realists

You know what a realist is? A realist today is a neurotic with an excuse for doing nothing.

The Time Is Now

There're a lot of things that you can do, but you've got to do what God has asked you to do, and stick to it!

You have all eternity to experience the presence of God, but you have a very short time to do something for Him.

The Theology of Risk

We have lost the theology of risk. There is an inner confidence that we've lost. We've lost zeal. We've lost guts. Unless you are willing to do the ridiculous, God will not do the miraculous.

Doing the Ridiculous

Remember old Abraham. He was ninety years old — ninety — when the Lord told him he would be the father of a great nation. God said, "Your descendents will be like sand on the seashore," and Abraham believed. I like to imagine Abraham, stooped with old age, outside his tent, working. A neighbor passes by and asks him, "Abraham, what are you doing?" The old man looks down and mutters to himself.

"What? I can't hear you!" the neighbor yells.

Finally Abraham looks up. "I'm making a cradle, okay?!"

Well, the neighbor is dying. "A cradle?" he says. "Boy, do you have hope."

But in Abraham's case, the impossible happened. You see, God expects His people to do the ridiculous so He can do the miraculous. And we are not willing to do it. But we must, even if we don't fully understand His commands.

Sitting Ready

After Jesus multiplied the loaves and fishes, the Scripture says, "He gave thanks and gave the bread to all who were *sitting ready*" (John 6:11). Today we are not sitting ready:

waiting for the Lord to give, to act, to inspire, looking at the Present Moment with the awe of a child. God's grace comes only to those who are sitting ready.

STEPPING OUT

In every instance, God waited on His apostles to step out in faith not knowing what was coming next, and this is where we fail today. We have been brainwashed to believe that we first must have a goal, then we must have a committee, then we must have meetings, and a fund drive, and then we must get qualified people and a budget, and then you can begin to do something for the Lord. By that time, you've forgotten what you started out to do.

COMFORT VS. HOLINESS

We're so worried about our image. We're so concerned about human respect that we smother the Spirit. We don't want to be considered fanatics, or too pious. But the pious may not necessarily make it, because the pious are so often scandalized by the ridiculous. Christ's way is for the strong, the gutsy. In Our Lord's time there were an enormous amount of good people but they did not accept Him because He was not *comfortable!* He did not easily fit into their way of life. Jesus is giving you such an opportunity to be holy, holier than all the saints that have ever been, because the world is in such need of shining lives, beacons to see by.

No Experience? No Training? No Problem

Mother Angelica never trained for any of the major occupations of her life. She was a cloistered nun who had never written extensively when she began churning out her mini books. She had absolutely no broadcast experience when she leapt into television production — in fact, she didn't even see television until the early 1960s during her first visit to Birmingham, Alabama. Mother didn't rely on her own gifts or skills, she charted a different path.

In the Old Testament, when it came time to build the Temple, the Lord said, I will give men talents in wood and gold and metal and embroidery that they may build My house. And the thought came to me, if God did it then, can He not do it now? Can He not give us talents that we do not possess when we use them for His kingdom? You bet He can, and He does.

THE RESULTS OF OUR WORK

We use the talents we possess to the best of our ability and leave the results to God. We are at peace in the knowledge that He is pleased with our efforts and that His Providence will take care of the fruit of those efforts.

MOTHER'S WRITING WORKSHOP

The author of fifty-three mini books on the spiritual life, Mother never anguished over her literary works. She wrote a paragraph at a time on yellow legal pads in her chapel. Like everything else about Mother, her writing process was unpretentious and practical.

You know what I do when I'm writing a book? I say, "Jesus, tell me what to write." And that's the next chapter. It's like a light goes on in my head and I write the thoughts that come. When the Lord stops sending thoughts, the book is finished. I think He's afraid of what would be on the page if He didn't come through.

GOD USES DODOS

God is looking for dodos. There are a lot of people who know it can't be done so they don't do it. But a dodo doesn't know it can't be done. God uses dodos. And I'm a dodo.

GOD WORKS WITH DUMMIES

I just want to show you how God works with dummies . . . An electrical engineer came and knocked on the door of the house we were staying at. He asked to speak with the supervisor. I said, "I'm the supervisor."

Then he says, "May I speak to the contractor." Men always give me that perplexed look.

I said, "I'm the contractor."

"Fine," he said. "Well, may I speak to someone who knows something about these plans."

I said, "I'm it, brother." You know the Lord honored my ignorance, because the only thing I really knew was the one thing wrong on the plans. I said, "You've got the receptacle in the wrong place."

He said, "Where?"

I said, "Right here." It was the only thing I knew. But he didn't know that, he still doesn't know it . . . and he never questioned me again.

THE STRENGTH OF THE WEAK

God will often grant to the very weak what the strong have refused. When a strong man refuses to obey God, He turns to the weak; they will give Him more glory.

Our Lord Himself said, when the apostles came back one day full of joy over the things they had accomplished for the kingdom, "I thank you Father of heaven and earth because you have hidden these things from the wise and prudent and revealed them to little ones." Does this indicate that God likes stupid people? No. Simple and weak people are so conscious of their inadequacies that they depend upon God and they face the truth; a truth that proclaims: "I can do all things in Him who strengthens me" (Phil. 4:13).

MONEY AND TRUST

When Mother Angelica was building her printing operation, she needed a camera. Placing a call to a local printing supply store, she asked if they had "a camera for dodos" in stock.

The man said it cost $4,500. I said, "I'll take it." I think we had ninety dollars that day. I figure when you don't have it, it doesn't make any difference anyway — you may as well order what you need!

My experience is: God gives you what you need as you need it. When we had bills for

$300 one week, $350 would come in. Usually, just what you need comes in — not much more — just what you need. Have faith.

No Need for Fear

We are trained today to fear. I'm not afraid of failure. Fear of failure is the worst thing in the world, because it prevents you from stepping out. For example, someone said to me, what will happen if you buy all this printing equipment and then you can't pay for it? I said, "I'll get a million books out of it before they take it back."

A Strategy for Building

Mother Angelica lacked the funds for every project she ever undertook, her monastery in Birmingham included. If she felt God was compelling her to some work, off she would go, pressing forward until further notice. What follows is the rationale for her approach.

Albert Moore is the contractor who built some of our buildings, and I told him one afternoon, "Albert, we're going to build this building."

"Do you have the money?" he said.

I said, "No."

"I don't understand," he said.

"We're going to build without money," I told him.

"That kind of makes me nervous. How are you going to do that?" he asked.

"I'll tell you what we'll do," I told him. "We'll just begin and if the Lord doesn't provide we'll stop, and we'll be that far ahead. If we stop with just the slab at least we've got a slab — which is more than we've got now."

See, we don't think like God. We've got to have the whole thing in place before we begin. Well, I never saw a building go up so fast. We didn't have any money. Most of the materials and labor were donated — God did the rest.

FOOLS FOR CHRIST

The following comes from 1980, a year before Mother would found and launch The Eternal Word Television Network (EWTN). She was fifty-seven years old at the time and plagued by various disabilities — not that that ever slowed her down.

You know what gripes me? That our beautiful Church, with all Her saints and spirituality, is not on satellite beaming down all that beauty and treasure coast to coast and

258

around the world. We're not willing to be dummies for God.

You know that the Scripture says we must be "fools for Christ's sake!" (1 Cor. 4:10). Oh, but we want to be safe, we want to be successful, we want to have assurance. That's the world. Look closely at the apostles and see them for the dodos that they are. They had big personalities and bigger tempers. They were jealous of one another. Peter's psychological profile is so bad you would not elect this man dogcatcher. Imagine a leader who panics in a crisis. But God knows that His grace is at its best in our weakness.

CONVERSATION WITH A LOAN OFFICER

When trying to begin her printing operation, Mother Angelica needed a loan. So she went to a Birmingham bank. She was mired in debt from the construction of her monastery at the time and had nothing but faith to commend her when she approached the loan officer.

He looked at me very condescendingly, as men do to women sometimes, and he said, "Mother, what are your assets?"

"If I had any do you think I'd be here?" I said.

Then he asked, "What is your monthly

income?"

I said, "I won't know till the end of the month."

"You expect me to make a loan on nothing but faith?" he said.

I said, "Yes."

He said, "I can't do it."

I said, "Pagan."

MOTHER'S WITNESS

Throughout her two-decade leadership of EWTN, Mother Angelica never permitted budgets, investments, or elaborate fundraising to keep the venture afloat. She wanted the organization to live hand to mouth, month-by-month, reliant on the generosity of her viewing "family." The network would be totally dependent on Divine Providence, and that reality would become its own witness.

The Lord wants us to witness to many things and one is: That those who work for God should have no coffers, no silver, and no gold. The second is: It is true that when you tithe your time to God He multiplies it (and your work) in ways you cannot imagine.

It Evolved

What began as a nun's homespun studio in a monastery garage, twenty-five years later would become the largest religious media empire on the planet. EWTN is now a world-wide phenomenon reaching hundreds of millions of people in places Mother could not conceive of at the start.

My life has been a life of faith, and I believe in my heart that I know when Jesus asks me to do something. So I only try to do what he asks of me. He is the one who leads the way and He moves one step at a time. I try to follow. He takes another step and I take one. That's why when people ask how did you get the network, I always say it evolved. Everything we've ever done evolved. It was never planned.

This is an act of God. Our witness is the total Providence of God. He led us, He provided for us, He protected us. No one can say that myself or any of these nuns could have accomplished this, because we couldn't. This work evolved as long as we kept up with God.

Sturdy Threads of Inspiration

Each day of my life Our Dear Lord has had freight cars hanging on to a hair of inspiration. A phone call, something you might as well have left alone, but on that little thought, that inspiration, was unbelievable things. The network is one, the shortwave radio network is another. I tell you this to let you know that you can trust God totally, no matter what happens. The more you trust Him, the more He will do.

FEAR OF SUCCESS

I tell you what I'm afraid of: success. I must have success in order to reach the world, but can I handle it? Will success so enrapt me that I will forget the Master? Shall the glitter and the glamour of lights and attention, block Him out? Will I forget my sinner condition and think only of praise? That you can be afraid of. But failure? Never.

Prayer is not to forget God in success. There are many giants in our own day who have fallen because God blessed them with success.

AFTER FOLLOWING GOD'S LEAD

The Lord has told me a couple of times, "When you have done all you have been asked to do, say: 'I am an unprofitable servant' " (Luke 17:10). That's in the Scriptures. You come out in the end with Him, and that's as it should be. You depend on God's grace. If there's any reward, it's

His grace; you don't need thanks.

**Prayer for Faithfully Following
Divine Inspiration**

Heavenly Father, give us that hope and joy that nothing can disturb. Lord Jesus, Eternal Word, pour into our hearts the kind of faith that moves mountains: the mountains of doubt, anxiety, and fear. Through the merits of Your precious Blood, remove all our hesitation and help us never forget our total dependence on Thee. Holy Spirit, we find Your will so puzzling at times, but we know Your paths and Your Commandments. Let us ever adhere to them and be receptive to the inspiration of each Present Moment. Amen.

13
MOTHERLY ADVICE
FOR THE FAMILY

When the matriarch of a family reunites with her children, it is customary to impart all sorts of far-flung wisdom and to address the problems confronted by the juniors. Below are Mother Angelica's ruminations on family life (including family strife), love, Sunday worship, and more. So, find a comfy place on the couch and listen to a few important words from your mother.

GOD'S RIGHTS

Only God has sovereign rights — no one else — and we refuse them today. People say, "No one has a right to tell me what to do." That attitude is the essence of pride, and it's very dangerous. God and His Church *do* have the right to tell you what to do.

CHRISTIANITY

Christianity is a living body whose head is Christ, and it throbs with love.

GOD IS LOVE

If God is love and you are called to be like God, then you too must love. Your every glance, your every movement, every word, must shout to those around you: Love. There is no suffering you can endure that He has not endured. No joy comes your way that He does not send. In all circumstances, pain or joy, it is the Lord. It is Love.

LEARNING TO LOVE

Allow people to love you as they must love you, not as you want them to love you. Even God does not love us as we wish Him to. Learning to love is learning to accept love as it comes.

DOING AND BEING

We are always worried about what people are doing rather than what they are *being.* The doing is in the will, the being is a revelation of the soul; a revelation of what we believe.

The Importance of Humor

Humor is a gift that Christians should be filled with. You must laugh at yourself so you are able to take your neighbor's faults with a grain of salt. Give him the privilege of being imperfect — just like you, sweetheart.

Is It the Lord?

My mother, Sister David, was ill and in bed, and I was getting ready to leave to speak to the National Council of Catholic Women. Sister David had a bird in her room, a little parakeet, and I said to the bird, "So long, Chico." And he said, "Sock it to 'em, Angelica."

"It's the Lord," I told David. She looked at me and said, "No, it's Sister Regina. She taught him that."

You know what the lesson there is? Careful what you attribute to the Lord. Sometimes it's just a bird squawking.

Avoiding Destruction

One of our saints, St. Vincent Ferrer, had a vision that the world was going to come to an end because of the wickedness of the people. So he wasn't going to wait. He went out and preached all over Italy and France, and performed many miracles.

One day, in a city that did not believe him, he stopped the funeral of a great prince who had died. He told them to open the casket, which they did. St. Vincent told the man in the casket, who had been dead for five days, "Rise," and he rose. Then he told the resurrected man, "Tell these people if what I say is true." The man said it was true.

News of this spread everywhere and people repented. Now we look back and say St. Vincent was a fraud, the vision he had was not true. But all prophecies of doom are conditional. That means: If and when people repent and become holy, there is no need for destruction.

THE FAMILY IN THE IMAGE OF THE TRINITY

The family is a beautiful image of the Trinity. The man is head and he resembles the eternal Father, and like the Father he is to protect, to provide, to create, and to understand. He is to be compassionate like the Father and full of mercy.

The woman is made to the image of Jesus, and like Jesus she is to be meek, loving, a means of reconciliation and gentleness. She has intuition. She has something a man doesn't have: she is intuitive.

The children are like the Spirit. As the

Spirit proceeds from the Father and the Son, so the children proceed from the husband and wife. Like the Spirit they are a power, a bond of union, joy, and love. We call this "family."

Now, when the one in the middle wants to be head or the children want to be head, we have a distortion of the family image made to the Trinity, and you cannot deviate from this plan of God! When you do, you have a monster in your family. That's why the families today are not what they should be.

Parents Following the Children

A queen visited America several years ago, and they asked what most impressed her about America. She said she was very impressed by how the parents obeyed the children! But you see, unless you are trained and taught what it means to be a Christian and your family understands their position before God, all are in danger.

Women and Holiness at Home

Some men come home and all their wives do is gripe. Poor guy's had a hard day at the office and he comes home for some respite, and you gripe and gripe, or you find fault with him in public. I have no patience with women who harass their husbands in public. Somebody walks up and says, "Oh, you look great." And she says, "You should see him in the morning." Someone compliments him and says, "You're so kind." And the Mrs. says, "Well, he's not very kind at home." No wonder. Then you'll recall something he did thirty years ago. Poor guy is drinking his juice and reading his paper and you come out with: "I'll never forget the time you . . . yah, yah, yah."

You girls have the idea that holiness is not meant for you. Contain the griping, compliment your husband when you want to flatten him — that's everyday holiness. And remember, if you don't make it to heaven, nobody's going to make it to heaven.

THE COMMUNAL PROPERTY OF MARRIAGE

I want you to look at 1 Corinthians 6:17: "Anyone who is joined to the Lord is one Spirit with Him." The essence of married life is to be one spirit, and God has called you to be one spirit with Him. Your body is not your own property. He's talking here about fornication. Your body is not your property to do with as you wish. You don't belong to yourself. If married couples would understand that he is not his own property and she is not her own property, there would not be divorces. When they become their own property, they are finished.

CORRECTING CHILDREN WITH LOVE

We have a tendency to punish or threaten people as a form of correction. Occasionally parents will come to me and relate the following: "I've been hollering at my kids and yelled at them and tried to tell them what to do and nothing happens. They don't pay any attention to me." Do you know why? They shut you off. They didn't hear you, because they just internally tuned you out.

They know that even though their correction is justified, there is a personal anger mixed in with it. And they are not interested in hearing it. Why? Because for that moment they have not felt loved. The best form of correction is love.

A SOURCE OF TROUBLE IN THE FAMILY

This is why you have trouble in your families: you want everybody to be like you, which is the best there is. Fathers want sons to be like them. Women want their husbands to be like them. A woman told me: "You don't have to live with that old grouch."

But that man is part of her sanctification. Let's hope she, and you, catch on.

A MOTHER'S VOCATION

A mother's vocation is complete when she freely gives her child to God.

FAMILIAL LOVE

There are people in your own family that you don't particularly like. You may have a sister or brother and you're very happy when they are eight hundred miles away. That's just as true in contemplative life. But, you see, we *have* to love these people. I have to see something else in these people besides their faults and weaknesses and personality quirks, or I'm not going to make it.

We have to make an effort to love. You shouldn't let another person decide whether you are happy or grouchy, and when you concentrate on the actions of others, how they act and how they don't act, you're lost. They're the same people all the time; the problem is your reaction to them. Love is what the Lord asks of us. If we must love even our enemies, imagine how we are expected to love our family members.

Go around the room and pick out three beautiful qualities in each member of your family. We do that in the monastery. The sisters will say, "Mother, you're generous, understanding, and loving." I say, "I can buy that." Then I began to wonder. I think, "Angelica, if you are all these beautiful things, how come you're impatient and have a hot temper?" And I began to reason, and I found that I am generous by nature, with things and my talents, but I was not generous with my time. If a sister came up to me and I was in a hurry, I would say, "What are you bugging me now with this trite little thing for?"

God had already planted into my heart a tool: generosity. When I worked on being more generous, that thing that I already am, I suddenly became patient. So point out the virtues of your family members — build on those, and the rest will fall away.

ENTRUSTING YOUR FAMILY TO GOD

In your family, trust your children to Jesus. I know the economy is bad and you worry about tomorrow and you worry about your investments. But you only have one investment: in the kingdom of heaven. When you

have Jesus in your heart, you can do all
things and overcome the entire world for
yourself and your children.

Bringing Children Back to the Faith

Discovered in the monastery archive, the following instruction demonstrates Mother Angelica's concern for the laity, even those who
have left the fold.

The first of my three concrete steps for
bringing our children and grandchildren
back to Christ are as follows:

1. *Pray for them unceasingly and confidently.* Your prayers will never go
   unheard, your tears will never go
   unheeded. If it seems like your
   sacrifices have no effect, then know
   for certain that God is using them
   in His own way to bring back someone, somewhere.
2. *Be a visible example of what Christ
   asks from the Church.* Your constant
   good example is the best encourage-
   ment you can give. Practice your
   faith and develop the virtues of
   perseverance and charity. These will
   give you Christ's peace in the midst
   of this turbulent world.

3. *Be open in discussing your faith.* Explain as honestly as you can — with examples from your own life — how your faith got you through some pretty difficult situations in the past and why we need it today.

Remember that God loves your children and grandchildren even more than you do, and He will pursue them to their last breath.

LITTLE PORTIONS

Mother Angelica liked to remind her sisters that St. Clare, the founder of their order, was only eighteen and her cofoundress fourteen when they began the female branch of the Franciscans. They took their vows in a little chapel rebuilt by St. Francis called The Portiuncula, meaning "a little portion."

God used little portions. Don't pin God down to anything. He can do what He wants, when He wants, how He wants, because these people made themselves, allowed themselves to be, little portions. We need to say with them, "Lord, I'm your little portion. I'm your Portiuncula. I'm this little cube. Use me."

We have a right to be what God made us to be. Everybody's talking about equal rights, but what about God's rights? That should be our concern. He has a right to make a woman do one thing and a man another. He has a right to ask you to love Him because He created you. You are His. Where are the voices crying in the wilderness to defend God's rights?

God can give a woman a talent to be an engineer or a doctor, and no one has a right to say she can't be that, because it is a God-given talent. I'm in that position myself. Here I am a cloistered nun who should be like the three monkeys: see nothing, hear nothing, and say nothing. I've said to the Lord 150 times, "Are You sure You know what You are doing? Why would You have me go out and talk to people — I'm not the one." And He keeps saying just mind your own business and go. So God sometimes gives women great things to do. To God there is neither male nor female. We're all equal to God. We have different functions, and this is the issue today: we're trying to switch functions. You cannot do that. Before God we are all capable of tremendous holiness, whether you are a man or a woman.

TEASPOON DESTRUCTION

If you look at the liberals throughout the years, you'll notice that they've got a lot of patience. They practice what I call "teaspoon destruction." They don't do anything too suddenly, they just change things a teaspoon at a time. By the time you wake up, there's a bucket of water falling on top of you and the floor is drenched.

THE TRADITIONAL ROMAN MASS

Latin was the perfect language for the Mass. It's the language of the Church, which allows us to pray a verbal prayer without distraction. See, the purpose of the Mass is to pray and to be associated with the crucifixion and with that glorious banquet that we partake of in Holy Communion. He is there. But so much is spoiled in the vernacular.

During the Latin Mass you had the missal if you wanted to follow it in English. It was almost mystical. It gave you an awareness of heaven, of the awesome humility of God who manifests Himself in the guise of bread and wine. The love that He had for us, His desire to remain with us, is simply awesome. You could concentrate on that love, because you weren't distracted by your own language. You could go anywhere in the world and you always knew what was going on. It was contemplative because as the Mass was going on you could close your eyes and visualize what really happened. You could feel it. You could look to the east and realize that God had come and was really present. The way it is today with the priest facing the people, it's something between the people and the priest. Too often it's just some kind of get-together, and Jesus is all but forgotten.

THE EUCHARIST

Every time I receive the Eucharist it is more God in me. The Lord Himself said, "If you do not eat the flesh of the Son of Man you will not have life in you" (John 6:53). Your capacity to receive grace grows each time you accept His Body and Blood. If you give God a pint jar, you can't expect Him to put the ocean in it. The Eucharist broadens your ability to receive grace.

THE EUCHARIST AND HUMILITY

The Lord put Himself in the Eucharist to give you the opportunity to be humble. One must be humble to see Him in that host. Love and childishness go together. And

Jesus took the terrible risk of being forgotten by all of humanity so that you could remember Him and see Him there.

UNITY WITH THE CLERGY

You need to be united to your parish priest, and I don't care who he is, what he is, what he does, or what he doesn't do. I've had people say, "Oh, but if you lived under my pastor, you wouldn't say that." Do you ever think what a sick heart he has? How lonely he is? What suffering he might have had in his life that made him what he is?

Then you gripe about the bishops. Do you ever realize the terrible responsibility of being a bishop? And no matter what you do, somebody is unhappy with you. You can't stand criticism on a little level; can you imagine what they endure? You need to develop a spirit of compassion so deep that it embraces the whole world. Laity and clergy must be united in spirit for the greater glory of God.

THE APOSTLES TODAY

The apostles wouldn't pass the seminary today. Heck, I doubt if they'd make it past the psychological screening.

SUNDAY BEST?

A holy person is a joy-filled person. Sit in your car in front of any church on Sunday morning. Watch them going in and coming out. The saddest-sack bunch of people you ever want to see! They're dragging their kids in, angry over the parking space. The sermon was too long. The church was too cold. They miss the whole point — and when it's over, that's the end of it. The grouching begins the minute they walk out the church doors — sometimes earlier.

LISTENING TO SERMONS

I never saw such a bored group of people as the looks of you all listening to a sermon. If I was the speaker, I would be so discouraged. Some of you are asleep, some of you are bored. It's distressing because you are not listening. Some of you should try some public speaking, and we'll respond the way you do at Mass. What an un-Christian attitude. You can't tell me you're listening when your eyes are closed and your face is taut. Don't shut off the Word, because you're going to miss a lot of graces in your life. Don't say, "I've heard all of this before." Listen to what the Spirit wants to say to you right now. How uncharitable you are, to sit there like a sphinx while the poor priest is talking.

Now, maybe you don't like his interpretation. Fine. You don't have to like it. There are a lot of speakers that I don't like. But there have been times where the worst speaker will say something that hits me like a rock. So please don't sit there with a Christian Science grin. Wake up and listen. Really listen! There is no sermon that you cannot get something out of. I don't care who gives it. It's not what they are saying. It's the Word! You need to ask only one question when that homily begins: "What is Jesus going to say to me today?"

BAD HOMILIES

After Mass one day a woman came to me complaining about a priest's homily. His preaching ability left something to be desired, but then it's the Word you listen to, not the way it's presented. So this woman was complaining and I asked her, "How much did you put in the collection?" She said, "A quarter." I said, "What do you want for a quarter, Bishop Sheen?"

Prayer Before a Sermon

Lord, I need something. My soul is open to the attacks of the enemy, of my own flesh, of the world. I need the Word. Give me Your Word today.

EVERLASTING LOVE

The Lord says, "I have loved you with an everlasting love." If you remember this one truth, you will find peace in your daily life.

MOTHER'S WISH

I wish you heaven.

A Franciscan Blessing

Each evening Mother Angelica blessed her sisters with the Franciscan blessing that follows. It is taken from the book of Numbers.

May the Lord bless thee and keep thee. May the Lord let His face shine upon thee, and be gracious to thee. May the Lord look upon thee kindly, and give thee peace. Amen.

14
THE LAST THINGS

Like your life, the end is what this little book is really about. The Eternal Perspectives that we started with had their origins here: in a firm understanding that all things, even our lives, come to an end. With that in mind, here are some of Mother's thoughts on the last things or, depending on your perspective, the first things.

PRAYERS FOR THE DEAD

Passing a cemetery, I once said to a companion, "I wonder how many people are dead in that cemetery?" She looked at me and said, "All of them." Smart aleck. Well, I knew all of them were dead, but I meant how many in that cemetery needed some help to complete their journey? Every time you pass a cemetery it's time for a little prayer: "Eternal rest grant unto them, O Lord."

There are all kinds of quick prayers that

we have in the Church that are for use in everyday life. It's just common sense that you hope some of them get out of purgatory. What happens if you get to purgatory and all these people look at you and ask, "Why didn't you pray for me?" And you'll say, "I didn't think about it."

Well, nobody's going to think of you either.

THE POWER OF THE SOUL

Whenever I go to a wake, I always put my hand on the person's chest. It's a beautiful meditation on death. That chest is like a piece of marble, cold as ice and hard like a rock. The doctor says it's rigor mortis. I don't care what you call it; it's like a rock. If you want to appreciate the power of your soul, next time you go to a wake, very gently touch the deceased's chest, and see what happens to this body that we take such good care of when the spirit leaves it. It's hard, cold, and motionless.

MOTHER'S GREATEST FEAR

I'm not afraid to fail, because I've always learned something when I've failed. I'll tell you what I'm afraid of — and when I think about it I break into a cold sweat — I'm scared to death of dying and having the Lord say to me, "Angelica, *this* is what you might have done had you trusted more." I'm petrified of that.

DYING WITH DIGNITY

One of my sisters, Sister Immaculata, had a very progressive form of cancer. She was only forty-five. You know what she said before she died? She told me, "All I want to do is to live, whatever time I have left, with Jesus and my sisters. I want to be able to say as I am dying, 'Thank you, Lord.' " That's dying with dignity and demonstrating holiness of life. We need to think of that.

NEAR-DEATH REALIZATION

In the summer of the year 2000, Mother Angelica experienced what she would later describe as a near-death experience. The event gave her a new perspective on dying, and an appreciation of its suddenness.

When you die, you are the love, the compassion, you had in life — that's all you've got. All the things we've had to suffer in recent years, all the frustrations, all the anxieties and anger over what we consider injustices — they were all gone. It didn't matter . . . I

had a deep awareness of God, a deep awareness that we do not have here a lasting city.
You don't want to die and have to face Him
being angry at someone or hateful, never
overcoming your passions and faults, because it's so quick. I never had anything
happen so quickly. Be ready.

ONE LAST CHOICE

We must be careful not to judge the final
destination of others. I believe God extends
His hand to the greatest sinner one last
time, somewhere between their last breath
and the time He snatches their souls from
their bodies. He gives them one last choice.
And don't forget this too: For a person who
has been in habitual sin all their life, it will
be very difficult for them to make that
choice the last time. But if you have acquired a habit of being good, being loving,
bearing the gifts of the Spirit, trying to
control yourself, then you don't have to
worry about that last moment. You will
automatically make the right choice. You
have lived your life in the kingdom, and it's
merely a matter of passing over.

THE FINAL JUDGMENT

God is not like Social Security, where they take the best ten years of your life and judge your pension by that. God doesn't think that way. It's absolutely necessary as I accumulate merit and grace that my will conform to that grace, because at death your will is set. I can't make another act of will toward God. I have no choice after that. So the height of my glory is dependent upon my degree of union with God at that point.

That's why the Church has said: "From a sudden death, deliver us." Because you don't have a lot of time. I've heard sisters say, "I'd like to die in my sleep." Not me. I mean, what would happen if I went to sleep and I was not perfectly conformed to God's will?

SEEING GOD FACE TO FACE

You men, let me tell you something. When the Lord, God the Father, sees you at that beautiful moment that we call death, when you see Him face to face, He will not ask you what you accomplished, what big home you lived in, what cars you drove, or how famous you were. He will say one thing to you: "As a father, were you compassionate and merciful and understanding as I am?

That was your mission."

And you women who are mothers and those of you who are single, He will not ask you what you had or accomplished either. He will ask you, "Were you like my Son Jesus: humble and obedient and loving?"

You Will Glorify God

The ultimate purpose for every human being is to give honor and glory to God, and at the end it will be so. You will either glorify His mercy by entering the kingdom of heaven, or you shall glorify his justice by entering the kingdom of hell. But either way, whether you know it or not, or like it or not, you will glorify God.

Heaven

Heaven is your real home. This is our testing ground, that's all. We were created by God to be with Him. That's why it's so important to say yes to God in everything. Let Him guide you. Ask Him to give you all you need to accept your way of life and to live it well. I know Our Lord will bless you. He already has.

Your Place in Heaven

When we get to heaven, there will be many empty seats and many empty mansions, and they'll stay that way forever because God has destined each of us for our specific degree of glory. My place in heaven is mine. No one else will ever use it or possess it or live in it. If I don't get there, it will remain empty.

Purgatory

God created me to go to heaven. His mercy allows me to go to purgatory. Purgatory is a place of love unfulfilled. You found out at judgment how much God loves you and how you failed to respond. Purgatory is not a place of despair and regret — at that point you're very sorry for all the opportunities that passed you by. You're also very grateful that God had such mercy on you. The inability to be with God is the greatest pain in purgatory, because that's all you really want. The good news is, eventually, you'll get to Him; there is an end to purgatory.

I've always thought that life is full of enough tiny things and big things to purify us. I never did believe that everybody was ultimately destined for purgatory. Many of the people in purgatory have high degrees of union with God in heaven once they're released. In other words, it doesn't mean that because you went to purgatory your degree of holiness is less. Some of them are destined for great, high degrees of glory.

There is true joy in purgatory. I am justly punished and chastised there. I have seen God and I know that I am on my way. It may take me a while, but I know I'll see Him. There's no assurance in hell. There's nothing there.

HELL

There is a hell, my friends. Don't let anybody tell you there isn't. What they say today is that God is so compassionate He will not put anybody in hell, and that is true. God does not put you in hell. You put yourself there, because your hearts become so hardened, so stubborn, and inclined to seek your own comfort. We can't blame God. We must look to ourselves.

Who can describe hell? Total absolute absence of God; a place of revenge; a place of hatred for God; a place where you are forever right, and God is forever wrong. There's no repentance, no joy, absolutely no love. The worst part about hell is you know it will never, never end, and you will never see the face of the Lord. So make your choice now. Here's a final sobering thought (maybe too final): Wherever you land, wherever you go, it's forever. So make it a good destination.

ETERNITY

I read a description of eternity one time that has always stuck with me. The writer imagined the world as an iron ball and every thousand years a bird came and sharpened his beak on that ball. And when that ball had been worn down to nothing, that represented one second of eternity.

A FINAL REMINDER

Remember, Jesus loves you. Live with Him in the Present Moment. His love is everlasting.

THE LAST WORD

Since there is no more time, and you and I may not pass this way again, I will ask the Spirit to touch your hearts and teach you all these marvelous things: how to live in the Present Moment, how to be at peace when distress is assailing you, how to love when you don't feel loved, how to always commune with God in the depths of your soul, and how to bear those beautiful gifts of the Spirit, always.

I love you, and God loves you more than you know.

ACKNOWLEDGMENTS

In typical Angelica fashion, this book was assembled during one of the most tumultuous periods of my life. In August of 2005, just after beginning work on this book, our family was blessed with a beautiful baby girl. Nine days later, Hurricane Katrina drove us from our home in New Orleans, forcing us to relocate to Birmingham for ten months. I must first thank Mother Angelica, who not only gave my family shelter during this awful time, but also provided us with spiritual insights that helped make sense of our plight. I have learned to truly live in the Present Moment, Mama!

To all my friends in Birmingham: Chris Edwards, Peter and Sharon Gagnon, Doug and Terri Keck, Lauren McCool, Father Mitch Pacwa, Ned and Lee South, Bill Steltemeier, Father Francis Mary Stone, Michael Warsaw, and the Nashville Dominicans of St. Rose Academy, thank you all for your hospitality and your warm embrace during our time in the Magic City.

I owe a special debt of gratitude to Mother Angelica and the Poor Clares of Perpetual Adoration at Our Lady of the Angels Monastery for trusting me with these incredible "lost teachings." The abbess and her vicar, Sister Mary Catherine, PCPA, who recognized the importance of this project from the very beginning, have my deepest thanks for their enduring support and affection.

Special thanks must also be accorded to four nuns: Sister Maria Consolata, PCPA, who collaborated with me throughout the arduous process of locating, and in some cases transcribing, many of the private and public lessons of Mother Angelica; Sister Mary Agnes, PCPA, who also generously flagged some of Mother's great one-liners; Sister Grace Marie, PCPA, who snapped the photo of the author and her editor that graces the book jacket; and Sister Margaret Mary, PCPA, for her vigilant attention to Mother and for her kindness toward me. May God reward you all.

I also thank Markie Works for letting me share her touching story in my introduction, Mary Ann Charles for helping to locate the cover photo, and Father William Saunders for casting his fine theological eye over the manuscript.

At Doubleday, my steadfast editor, Trace Murphy, is responsible for making this book the jewel that it is. His unfailing good cheer and dedication to every detail made working on this project a joy. My visionary publisher, Bill Barry, instantly saw the importance of this work and has been its champion from day one. They are simply the best in the business. Thank you, gents.

Were it not for my spirited agent, Loretta Barrett, I would probably be on a stretcher at this point. She and her devoted comrades, Nick Mullendore and Gabriel Davis, have shepherded me through the thorny world of publishing with dedication and real caring. Thank you, my friends.

Deep gratitude and affection go to my parents, Lynda and Raymond, who kept the home fires burning during our exile from New Orleans. Finally, to my wife, Rebecca, who endured so much this past year, held our family together, and still found it in her heart to let me spend more nights and weekends with Mother — you are so cherished. I love you.

ABOUT THE AUTHORS

Mother Angelica established Our Lady of the Angels Monastery in Birmingham, Alabama, in 1961, and twenty years later founded The Eternal Word Television Network, which has grown into the largest religious media organization on the planet. Her *Mother Angelica Live* remains one of the most popular programs on the network and has made her an internationally beloved spiritual figure. She lives in her monastery in Hanceville, Alabama.

Raymond Arroyo, author of the *New York Times* bestseller *Mother Angelica,* is the news director and lead anchor of EWTNews. As creator and host of the news magazine *The World Over Live,* he is seen in more than 100 million households each week. He has worked at the Associated Press and the *New York Observer,* and for the political columnist team of Evans and Novak. His work has appeared in the *Wall Street Journal, The New Yorker,* and many other publications. He lives in northern Virginia with his wife and three children.